THE ONE RIGHT VIDEO

An Entrepreneur's Guide to Grow Your Community, Get More Qualified Leads, and Close More Sales Using YouTube

DIANA GLADNEY

A Simpler Way to Planning & Creating Videos That Convert!

Save time optimizing your content for success without feeling lost and all over the place trying to plan your content by yourself.

FREE VIDEO PLANNING GUIDE

Readers who use The Video Planning Guide alongside this book implement the strategies faster to create videos that convert.

Download The Video Planning Guide Free here:

https://OneRightVideo.com/VideoPlanningGuide

Published by Video Simplified Publishing.

02232023

Want to check out my recommended camera gear? Learn more at https://Diana.Link/Gear

For more video tips and advice, subscribe to the Diana Gladney YouTube channel: https://Diana.Link/YouTube

Print ISBN: 979-8-9875682-1-7

e-book ISBN: 979-8-9875682-0-0

Audiobook ISBN: 979-8-9875682-2-4

1st edition, February 2023

To My Mother & Father

Thank you for the never-ending belief you've had in me from childhood to today. You've helped mold me into the woman God created me to be, and I'm forever grateful.

To Auntie Shirley R.R.

Thank you for teaching me to push beyond "good enough" to uncover my best and beyond by helping break the calluses around my mindsets to expose what's possible with the right mindset. You changed my life.

To My Mentor Ray Edwards:

I cannot thank you enough for being a continuous guiding light that shows me daily that no matter what crosses we bear in life, we still have a purpose we can achieve; no matter what. Thank you for teaching me true perseverance.

To Heather Torres:

Thank you for inspiring me and your constant words of wisdom and guidance, and for believing in me. I cannot express my sincere gratitude for your love and guidance. Thank you so much.

For Mr. Robert Edwards

You'll never know the full impact you had on a group of rambunctious kids with raw musical talent. You helped to not only refine our sound, but pierce through our hearts and affirm to us daily who we could become. Thank you for your patience, love, and guidance.

Contents

Learn & Do.

Whatever you learn, go, and execute on it.

~ Diana Gladney

Foreword

I have the privilege of presenting to you a work of business brilliance, written by none other than my dear friend, Diana Gladney. Allow me to shed light on the person behind these pages and the qualities that make her truly remarkable.

In my years of acquaintance with Diana, I have come to know her as a steadfast believer in evidence-based practices, a paragon of efficiency, and a harbinger of results. In a world where mediocrity is often the norm, Diana stands out as a beacon of industriousness, conscientiousness, and an unwavering eye for detail. She possesses a work ethic unlike any I have encountered, and her unrelenting pursuit of excellence is an inspiration to us all.

But it is not just her tireless spirit that sets her apart. Diana is also a person of integrity, a trait that is all too rare in our current age. You can trust her implicitly, for she is a woman of her word and you can always count on her to have your back. Whether you are embarking on a new venture or navigating the stormy seas of life, you can rest assured that Diana will be there to lend a hand and see you through.

It is with great honor and pleasure, then, that I commend to you this book, written by such a remarkable individual. Within its pages, you will find a wealth of knowledge and insights that will leave you invigorated and inspired. However, I would be remiss if I did not caution you - this book is not for the faint of heart.

It is a call to action, a rallying cry for those who are not content to simply read the words but are eager to put them into practice.

For those of you who are ready to heed the call, I implore you to read this book with an open mind and an open heart. Embrace its teachings, put them into action, and watch as your life and business transform before your very eyes. But beware, for if you do not take action, you may find yourself on the receiving end of Diana's legendary tenacity and unwavering resolve. For she is not one to be trifled with, and those who underestimate her will soon find themselves regretting it.

Now, Constant Reader, I invite you to embark on this journey with me, to bask in the brilliance of Diana Gladney, and to experience the transformative power of her words & wisdom. You will not be disappointed.

Read this book, but most importantly, take action on what you read.

The future is yours for the taking.

To Your Prosperity,

Ray Edwards

Best-Selling Author of *How To Write Copy That Sells* and *Read This Or Die!*

Preface

I used to think that one day, I would live out the image in my mind of myself as an important corporate professional, helping to create change in people's lives.

However, I never dreamed it'd happen this way.

It had been three years since I had recovered from major surgery. Waking up to be told that I would battle with a disease that I couldn't get rid of changed my perspective of what I wanted to achieve in life.

Before the surgery, I lived every day in the worst pain I had ever felt. However, I still entered each day with the hope that one day my life would grow to be one of success, and that I would live a life that was meaningful and full of purpose. So far, that day had not yet arrived, but I remained hopeful.

I would start every day the same way: by making strong Colombian roast coffee, arguing with God during my drive to work (which I called prayer), and walking into my job, hoping that no one would say more than a simple "Good Morning" so that I could absorb myself in my work and start my ritual of listening to a book or training on my phone.

I had lost my desire to climb the corporate ladder after seeing friend after friend and coworker after coworker get laid off, fired, or quit. The Fortune 50 company that I thought would be the best job for me became a daily reminder of just how much I had grown to hate my life. I had begun to climb a ladder only to realize that it was on the wrong wall.

Like many companies that were recognizing that they were in a severe financial downward spiral and trying to prevent more people from leaving, they did what they always did: offer a pizza party instead of better raises.

Today was no different from any other day at the office. It was starting to feel like a ghost town, so it was very quiet when an all-too-familiar email popped up on my computer announcing that the pizza would be delivered by noon. I always felt that these pizza parties were a double-edged sword, subliminally saying, "We want to show appreciation, but not enough to give everyone normal raises. So, here's a pizza instead."

I was always grateful for these kinds of days. That is until my supervisor's boss decided to take another one of her famous write-up strolls. Clipboard in hand, she'd look for any little thing someone was doing to write them up to add to the ever-growing list of vacant cubicles in the office. She'd finally made it to my team's section and begun looking for something to add to her handy dandy clipboard.

"Hey, Diana, how are you?" Nancy said without ever looking me in the eye or even glancing at my face.

Instead, her head bobbed and weaved as if she was in an invisible boxing match, only looking at my desk for something to write me up about.

Seeing what had drawn her attention, I flatly responded, "Fine, Nancy. And you?"

It's probably a good thing she wasn't looking at my face because if she had, she would have seen my twisted frown calling her out on the false sentiment surrounding her apathetic inquiry about my well-being, which was clearly of zero interest to her.

"Good," she said, walking away with another practiced response.

She didn't find anything to add to her clipboard, and it was then she finally met my eyes. Now, I was angry. I was annoyed for the rest of the day. Just like that, I went from being in a good mood and able to deal with another day at the bank to remembering why I had grown to hate this job. That night at home, I broke my own rule of not bringing work stress into my house, but I just couldn't shake the thought that if this was what my life was going to look like, I was done.

Something had to change. That next morning, I didn't have my usual prayer and couldn't work.

The clock went from 7:15 a.m. to 8:15 a.m. and I still couldn't get any work done. I had only emailed a handful of clients and sat staring at my computer screens. I texted my friend, complaining about my job and life, but instead of encouragement, she replied, "Well, if you're that frustrated and believe God is calling you to do something else, quit, but don't keep complaining about it if you're not going to do anything about it. Either quit and trust God or keep working that job. Didn't you tell me we're getting too old to keep playing with God? Quit then." Her words hit me like a ton of bricks, and something shifted in me.

I paid my bills and found myself doing something I only did at home - I looked into my eyes and prayed aloud, "God, if this is you telling me to quit and trust you, let me know. I'm dying in this job and can't keep living like this. If this is all I'm going to do, you could have taken me when I was on the surgery table. I didn't need to wake up, suffer with a disease I can't get rid of, and work a job I hate."

I stood there, looking into my own eyes, hoping for some kind of sign that what I was about to do was right, instead of what seemed like an emotionally charged and illogical decision. I don't remember how long I stood there, but surprisingly, no one ever walked into the bathroom during this entire dialogue, which was unusual.

I walked out of the bathroom with one thing on my mind. In a state of disbelief, I began cleaning out my desk. I placed company documents in the huge shredder bin and cleared my computer of both company and personal documents. I placed all my belongings in a shopping bag I had on my desk, and then my supervisor emerged from the bathroom I had just left an hour prior.

"Hey Nicole, my badge and keys are on your desk. Can you badge me out? I'm resigning," I said.

"Okay? Is everything all right?" she asked, shocked and in disbelief.

"Yep, I just need to grab my things from my desk," I replied as I walked toward my desk to retrieve my two bags and jacket.

When my desk came into view, my supervisor could tell from the expression on my face that I was serious and not joking like I usually would. During the walk to the exit, she repeatedly tried to offer me ways to take time off to reconsider, but my response remained the same: "What would be the point?"

Thankfully, I had my camera with me that day, and I knew that the title of my Friday live stream on my YouTube channel would be "Quitting My Full-Time Job to Go Full-Time in My Business!"

I share this story with you because when people see the transition my life has made from this day to the day you're reading this book, they often think it was a well-planned scheme, but it wasn't. I quit my full-time job with benefits, no savings, and only $96 in my bank account, with no immediate prospects for paying my bills.

I'm not saying that this is the right choice for you, and I don't suggest that you do the same. Nevertheless, I will say this, through God's grace and by leveraging the skills I developed since 2016, creating videos while working full-time at a bank, I've become a full-time video marketing coach, author, speaker, and entrepreneur on YouTube.

Honestly, you can achieve anything you want to learn and make any connections you desire through online video.

I'm sure that, like many other entrepreneurs, you're picking up this book because you have a vision you want to achieve.

As we dive deeper into each chapter, I'll reveal tactical principles that you can implement right away in your business and brand. YouTube is unique among social platforms, and even if you only know how to use a smartphone, you can create simple and effective videos that can dramatically change your life.

Throughout the book, we'll explore the mindset shifts you'll encounter when you enter the world of content creation, how to buy gear without wasting money, and the frameworks I still use today to create "The One Right Video."

"The One Right Video" isn't about accidentally creating a one-time viral video and trying to build a business around it, but about creating a video framework that will serve your business and share your vision with the world.

Each chapter will end with "Creator Next Step" cards to help you apply what you learn and start seeing results right away.

Let's begin and show you how to create "The One Right Video."

The One Right Video Can Transform Your Life

I had just hung up from speaking with my business coach and I couldn't believe I just agreed to create a video and post it online. Of all the things I expected him to say, that was the last thing I wanted to hear.

Instantly, my mind started racing with a million and one thoughts.

- What settings should I use?
- Should I use the front camera or the rear camera on my phone?
- Where should I record this video?
- Is this going to make me look like a fool?
- How many people are going to see this video if I post it to YouTube?

The thing that was bothering me wasn't that I had agreed to do one video, but thirty videos!

Around the time I created my 20th video, something interesting happened. I logged into YouTube to upload my newest video and I saw the previous video had skyrocketed from the normal three to seven views from me, my coach, and some accountability partners to over 100 views!

I was blown away!

I instantly knew I had uncovered something amazing with YouTube when one viewer commented that he was looking for someone else's video but instead found mine.

I pondered this singular statement for days. Something was different about YouTube and I was determined to find out how this platform worked.

I knew that if I could understand how to make videos that attracted my target audience and were interesting enough that they'd actually enjoy watching the video, I could actually have success on YouTube much faster than trying to crack the crazy code of Facebook. While it was an awesome platform, it wasn't a search engine people naturally went to searching for content.

Nearly all the other social platforms are places people find you from ads, recommendations, shares, or something else that sent people to your profile before you natively gained traction.

YouTube, however, was different.

People went to YouTube to see how to do something or to learn more about topics they were interested in. I knew that if I could get 100 people to accidentally find my videos on YouTube, I could uncover how to create videos for my target audience and grow my business leveraging YouTube.

One hundred people may not sound like a lot of people, but imagine giving a talk and the room was packed to standing room only because there were 100 excited guests waiting to hear what you have to say.

Imagine your message and your brand reaching numbers the equivalent to the population of major cities like New Orleans of 300,000+ or your channel reaching the equivalent of American states or more!

Realizing that behind these numbers are real people puts your potential reach in a whole new light.

I've created over 1,000 videos across various social platforms, quit my job at the bank while well under 1,000 subscribers, and have since grown my channel to over 1.5 million views and growing!

Through leveraging YouTube and learning to create engaging videos, I've been able to create and build a life I'm proud of that helps change people's lives. I've worked with incredible brands like Ecamm Live, Google, Sony, Amazon, and Adobe. I've had the honor of speaking on incredible stages like Social Media Marketing World and for the number one motivational speaker in the world, E.T. The Hip Hop Preacher.

If you're anything like I was and you see the vision of how powerful YouTube can be for your business and your brand, all you need is The One Right Video to completely change your life.

Like many entrepreneurs waking up to the realization that video and social media were, without a doubt, the new staple for any successful business, I discovered that it doesn't come without the fear, frustration, and anxiety around how to actually create online video content that's not ongoing boring promotional content.

From basic starter searches on Google, reading tons of blog posts, 1.5x podcast listens, and of course, skipping, scanning, and scrolling through countless videos on YouTube, it's frustrating to still not have the clear and concise answers you desire about how to create good, competent videos for the average entrepreneur on YouTube.

Many entrepreneurs question if YouTube is saturated or if it's too late to get started on YouTube.

With the advancements of the modern-day smartphone and a free Gmail account, everyone has the ability to create a video and upload it with one device that's probably less than three feet from you now.

The problem isn't a saturated market, the validity of YouTube, or that there are over 500 hours of video uploaded to YouTube every minute[1]. It's the quality of the content that attracts your ideal viewer to your content like bees to honey.

There's never been a better time to create videos on YouTube because more people are coming online every day and there are new generations of users always on the hunt for answers.

The problem will be finding great, quality, and relevant content.

The problem isn't how many videos pop up daily in your niche if they aren't compelling enough to capture and keep your audience's attention and if you're not showing up as your target audience's go-to resource in your niche.

While an abundance of excellent videos on filmmaking, photography, and videography are accessible, none of those quite address the specific and unique concerns of what to buy, how to use it, and how to craft great and attractive video content your target audience will binge-watch specifically for entrepreneurs; without feeling like you need to become a filmmaker to create amazing videos for your brand.

It is my deepest desire to help you, dear reader, to create a significant impact in your brand and business for the people that need what only your unique message can offer.

I used to create videos that didn't look or sound how I imagined they would.

I was not getting traction and attention from the right target audience and questioned how could videos that looked substandard attract the right audience.

WHAT WE'LL COVER IN THIS BOOK

In this book, I will break down the recipe of content strategies most beneficial and successful for entrepreneurs transitioning into content creation, whether you have a brick-and-mortar business or if you offer products and services primarily purchasable online.

The chapters outlined in this book are uniquely focused to take you through the five essential phases of transitioning into a content-creating entrepreneur.

- **Phase 1** | The Mindset of a Content-Creating Entrepreneur
- **Phase 2** | Maximizing Your Time to Create Engaging Videos
- **Phase 3** | Camera Gear & Technology Simplified
- **Phase 4** | Video Content Creation Strategies
- **Phase 5** | Video Marketing Strategies

Throughout these five phases, you'll want to keep top of mind who your ideal target viewer is, the specific and unique pain points your videos will solve, and the types of videos you intend to create on your YouTube channel.

Even as a skilled technician in your creative field, adopting the mindset of a creator comes with all new challenges and hurdles. Once we address the elephant in the room and what dishes you should NEVER serve to your community on YouTube, I'll expose everything you need to know to craft videos for your brand that your target viewer will binge-watch!

Throughout this book, I'll teach you the unique recipe any entrepreneur can leverage, including:

— My C.L.A.R.I.T.Y. Content Framework, the bulletproof video system to ensure videos are clear and serve the intended target audience their desired outcome and do their job.

— 4 Keys to Craft Killer Intros That Capture & Keep Their Attention.

— 5 Stage Video Framework for Crafting Simple & Engaging Educational Content.

— Embedding My Special Secret Sauce Elements of Storytelling.

— How to Build a Content Creation Team to partner creatively with you so that you can focus on your clients and running your business, and they can focus on bringing your video ideas to life with no micromanaging included.

Through leveraging the skills I've learned and developed over half a decade of creating video content for my brand, I'll show you how to implement the Learn & Do principles I have developed. If you can commit to taking one solid focused effort with limited distractions—AKA avoid TikTok for a little bit—and I'll teach you in this book how to easily create *The One Right Video.*

The One Right Video will expand the reach of your brand from a local market to a global audience on YouTube.

The One Right Video will turn viewers into customers.

The One Right Video will open the door to stages you've dreamt of speaking on to share your message and your brand.

The One Right Video will expose the ideal clients to your brand to not only sell your products and services but to impact and change their lives.

The One Right Video will transform your life.

Not just create a small or sometimes larger change in what you're doing but truly *transform* your life.

I believe your brand has significant value to add in your niche and your unique message shouldn't be absent from showing up on YouTube. In fact, I believe your brand can have a critical impact and change the world with YouTube.

I want to take you on the journey to creating better videos that amplify your brand because *The One Right Video* can change your life!

So, let's get started!

Phase 1 | The Mindset of a Content-Creating Entrepreneur

Chapter 1

Doubt is a Distraction

All distractions are equal.

When you decide you're going to become a video content creator, you easily find yourself surrounded by fellow content-creating entrepreneurs. Such was the day when I chatted on a call with my friend, and she shared with me some concerns and doubts she had about releasing some new content on her YouTube channel and even some things in her business.

The conversation quickly turned from the typical what we were up to, to the other end of the phone, oozing with doubts and concerns. They were legitimate concerns, but full of fears and doubts.

However, instead of just saying the typical, "Oh, it'll be alright" or "Man, that's messed up. I hope things get better," I told her, "Why don't we do a little exercise I like to call 'discrediting the devil'."

When you make the decision that you want to share your vision using video to help amplify your brand and business, outside of the normal questions of what gear to use or how social platforms like YouTube work, and so forth, it's not long before you're quickly drifting into "incognito searching" your competitors to see how they're doing.

From 50,000 subscribers, 250,000 subscribers, 1 million subscribers and all kinds of variations of follower counts in between, there are competitors that are doing well for themselves, and it's easy to let doubt creep in.

Then the real questions settle in, and you might begin saying to yourself:

- Should I even waste my time?
- Can I really do this?
- Will this be another attempt I add to my list of failures?

These are all legitimate concerns that *have* to be addressed if you're going to journey through the transition from an entrepreneur to a content-creating entrepreneur. And even after you've created videos, you will need a strong mindset to debunk on the odd day a bad actor leaves you a negative comment.

It boils down to one fundamental belief that you can't be convinced of, but have to fully and firmly believe in your heart that **your vision deserves to be shared with the world.**

Socking the Devil in the Jaw

By nature, I'm not a violent person, but when it comes to belief systems, it's a different ball game. I believe in declaring all-out war on doubts, disbelief, and distractions.

While on this call with my friend, I shared with her that one of the best ways I combat moments of doubt is by testing the validity of them to see if there's anything I actually need to course-correct, or if these thoughts and associated feelings I'm having are unjust distractions from the opposition trying to create distractions for me.

That's when I decide it's time to get violent and aggressive, and do what I call discrediting the devil and essentially sock him square in the jaw to shut his mouth.

Is this even necessary, or is this some overzealous reaction to temporary emotions from experiencing temporary defeat?

Let's revisit some common doubts new creators have when getting started on YouTube and creating video content:

— Am I good enough?

— How long will this take to grow?

— I don't even know what I'm doing!

— Will people even watch my videos?

— My channel is not as good as XYZ's YouTube channel...

Most of these concerns are rooted in very specific and identifiable fears and negative associations. Some are potentially valid, and some are not.

I've worked with entrepreneurs and brands with massive organizations and businesses that still have succumbed to these very same concerns.

So, is it overreacting? Not at all!

I believe entrepreneurs and content creators are the Renaissance artists of our time, but when plagued with fear, doubt, and distractions from the many voices online and on social media, it's easy to discredit the vision and purpose I believe lives inside all of us because it's quickly drowned out with this digital noise.

In this book, I am going to teach you my 7-Step C.L.A.R.I.T.Y. Framework to make sure you're creating excellent video content that stands out from the masses on YouTube and, like a laser, homes in on your target audience to convert viewers into customers, and customers into loyal fans of your brand.

"All distractions are equal." ~ Diana Gladney

The Battle of Belief Systems

In the Bible, there's one story that I've always found interesting, and it's the story of David and Goliath. We're all familiar with it.

What's interesting is these two guys actually have a lot in common because they both believed:

— they could win this battle of single combat against one another;

— their army would take over the land, conquering their enemy;

— and they both had hope that they'd win and live to see another day.

The reason we all really remember this story regardless of our beliefs is not because of how much these two had in common, but because the **difference in character and experience** each had were worlds of difference apart.

And to boot, Goliath was a freaking giant! Literally, a towering, massive giant, and David was a meager shepherd boy who played the lyre. Poor Dave wasn't intimidating anybody in that getup.

Everything was lined up perfectly for David to fail and Goliath to win. Everyone on BOTH SIDES would have been confident in making the bet that David would lose.

Side Note: Imagine being on a battlefield, and you're headed out to do battle against a giant and ZERO people believe in you. Not even your own people on your side are showing a little care to lie to you to pump you up even a little. Geeze.

When you're consumed with doubts, doubled down and amplified, looking to see who's already having success in your industry or niche, you're basically deciding to stand in the middle of an active battlefield with no armor yet, hoping to make it home safely.

It's not likely to happen.

It takes courage to actually address what you're feeling and thinking and where this uncertainty may be coming from. One thing will always remain true, regardless if your concerns are valid or not, and that's that all distractions are equal.

And THAT is why David won and not Goliath.

David wasn't distracted by the fears of others around him or the distraction of the real-life giant in front of his face. His belief was bigger than his present circumstance.

The same has to be true for you when you do your inevitable incognito searching, and you see how well others in your niche are doing. Don't get distracted by that. There is still an audience and community of people waiting to see your videos.

It reminds me of a video I didn't think I needed to make on my YouTube channel because there were already what I thought great videos on the topic. That is, until a community member reached out and asked why I hadn't created this particular camera video yet. I shared why and even referred to some fellow creators' videos.

I quickly received the nicest reply to show me how wrong I was, simply stated, "Yeah, but they're not you. I want to learn to use my camera from you. *You* get me, Diana."

Enough said. I made the video.

Now, nearly 50,000 other viewers agreed with that same sentiment because that video exploded on my channel with heart-warming comments that shared that same belief.

Remember, all distractions are equal.

Equal to keeping you away from your goals, dreams, and the aspirations you desire.

When the fears, doubts, and frustrations begin to creep up on you, you have to discredit that little devil sitting on your shoulder who is speaking nonsense, which, if you're not careful, you'll believe.

To discredit the devil, you need to ask yourself:

1. Are these concerns based in some truth that is hard for me to handle at the moment?

or

2. Are these concerns based in fears and doubts I have of myself that have no basis of validity at all, but I just *feel* like they do?

Let's revisit and break down these concerns one by one and actually address them to break apart the callused shell from around your mindset, layered with doubts and limiting beliefs that keep you majoring in the minor.

Or, said a different way, focusing on the small unimportant details versus those that are actually worthy of your attention.

Addressing Your Limiting Beliefs

"Am I good enough?"

- You haven't actually taken any actions in a completely new environment and field yet, so this doubt is unfounded and not worthy of your attention. How can you be good or bad, for that matter, at something you've never done? Dismiss this one.

"How long will this take to grow (or build)?"

- Creating anything of value takes time. Commit for the long haul, or accept early on whether you truly believe your vision deserves to be shared with the world.

"I don't know what I'm doing!"

- Of course you don't; you've never done it before. This is not a problem; this is a fact of anything brand new to you. Creating great video content is learnable. **All skills are learnable.**

"I don't know how to use all this camera gear. I'm not tech-savvy."

- Again, not a problem. Learning video is a skill, like driving. All skills are learnable. You put your life in your hands daily by driving—a camera won't kill you.

"Will people even watch my videos? I don't know the first thing about creating videos or how to start one."

- Valid point. You must first create the videos people want to watch; guessing if a video is good enough doesn't serve you or your potential viewers.

The difference is, through reading this book, you will have a strategic approach to creating your video that will give you the framework to create videos your audience loves and appreciates.

Learning to change your language from ***"I don't know how to..."*** to ***"I'm in the process of learning how to..."*** is the great bridge builder to having success with your video content.

Remember, **all skills are learnable.**

CREATOR NEXT STEPS

- [ ] Write out your top distractions. What are limiting beliefs you've had about creating video content?
- [ ] What's a simple step you can take today to discredit the limiting beliefs you've written down?

Chapter 2

Toxic Video Creator Beliefs

Constantly stretch your belief systems.

When I found my first paid mentor, of course, through YouTube, one thing he had me create was a free offer (aka a freemium or premium free offer) that would help me build an email list.

So, I created a super short personal development audio program, attached it as a free offer so when people subscribed they'd receive the program, and it actually received some great feedback that people were receiving value from it.

As I began taking on new clients, one thing I realized was that every single new client had limiting beliefs. From working with solo entrepreneurs, established corporations, or nonprofit organizations all over the world to leverage YouTube to amplify their brand, guess what?

No matter how large their organization was, they still had limiting beliefs if YouTube would really work for them.

If you don't uncover what your true limiting beliefs are right now, *before* you start creating content, you're going to find yourself with Creative Constipation. That's the cousin of procrastination. (FYI, that whole family is jacked up.)

I don't care how many years you've been in business, how successful you've been in other avenues with your brand, EVERYONE has these little toxins on the shelf, ready to ruin any content you try to dish out. And you need to defeat them now, or they'll catch you off guard at your weakest moment, and derail or dismantle your channel.

Then you'll end up like the unfortunate would-be creators in my email and DMs, telling me it's been over a year since they purchased "all this gear" recommended on YouTube and haven't created a single video.

Don't be that person.

The 3 Most Toxic Limiting Beliefs

1. ***"My brand is unique. No one is doing what I'm doing."***

This couldn't be further from the truth.

It's not that you can't have a unique spin on a particular solution or niche, but if you believe your brand is a true unicorn, you can't expect to find the rest of your mythical unicorn community.

One night in 2021, I sat on my phone aimlessly scrolling through TikTok looking for the next unexpected funny video, or to learn something from a hashtag I follow, like #ContentCreators or #YouTubeCreators—you know, something normal.

Of course, the "For You" page on TikTok recommended the most bizarre thing I'd ever seen—people trying mustard, regular ol' mustard you'd put on a sandwich, on watermelon. This is pretty much a war crime on condiments and fruit.

As wild as it sounds, there are people who have eaten watermelon with mustard on it and swear it's delicious!

There's a whole community of people who now love to do this. I blame TikTok for the growing popularity of this bizarre trend, but even if it's your first time hearing this crazy combination, there are some people that enjoy or at least have tried this bizarre food combo. So, while it's different to say the least and something you wouldn't expect, there's still an audience for it online.

So, as you can see, no matter how different your brand's content can be, there is still an audience online that will love what you create.

There's still an audience for you on YouTube, TikTok, or any place online where you can share your vision using video.

2. ***"My niche is already too crowded."***

Let's unpack this for a moment.

If you're at least 30 years old, remember the days of being a kid and walking through malls and stores like Sears during Christmas and seeing how packed the appliance section would be?

As an adult, I now fully understand the joy my mother and father had looking at the features of a new washing machine, stove, or refrigerator. But back then, I thought it was the most boring area of any store ever!

"Why even display these humongous things taking up all this floor space anyway?" I'd think to myself.

These major appliances were on display because ***people were buying them***!

It's simple!

I believe attention is the number one most traded commodity online, and that's what your first goal is with your ideal viewers, to **get their attention**.

It's no different from those huge appliances lined up in Sears so that when you entered the store, the appliance ***commanded*** your attention and encouraged you to open it up! See what it's like, imagine having one of these for yourself.

That foot traffic has now become online viewers, and the goal is the same as it was in the store: *get their attention.*

If people are still buying sofas, living room sets, refrigerators, and dishwashers, despite those purchases lasting upwards of a decade or longer, there's no such thing as "too crowded" for audiences already rip-roaring and ready to watch and be transformed by content like you're going to create.

3. "There are too many experts already. I won't matter." or *"Does my voice even matter?"*

This is another way people will often phrase this limiting belief, and it boils down to **not feeling worthy or good enough**.

I'm the youngest of six in my family, and that's like me saying, "I don't think I'll get to eat because I'm the youngest."

That statement has nothing to do with being born last, but the fear of *feeling* last, unimportant, and ignorable. Thankfully, I never did feel that as a kid, and there was always plenty to eat.

When you're positioning your brand on YouTube, comparison syndrome always tends to rear its ugly head. Comparison is the thief of joy, and **you can control this**, so stop it!

Like right now, stop it!

You are good enough as you are today.

Right now, the current version of you that is reading this book.

You don't need to compete because there is a community of people waiting, longing, and desiring to hear YOU.

How do I know?

Because I get comments all the time from people saying how glad they are that they've *"finally"* found a channel like mine. That they've been wishing a channel like mine existed, and *"Finally, a black woman in tech talking about cameras that look[s] like me? Instant subscriber!"*

I've received comments like these and many more like them that, despite the millions of channels and many millions of views on videos on the internet and YouTube, my channel was the one that their heart longed to see but couldn't find until I showed up.

You are enough as you are today to make changes in people's lives with your brand and business. You don't need to be like the existing voices in your niche.

Your target audience needs YOU.

You need to be **you** because that's what the world is truly thirsting for.

Your voice, your message, and your vision are important to the world.

CREATOR NEXT STEPS

- [ ] Write out your top three toxic video creator beliefs that you've thought about yourself.

____

____

____

- [ ] Write out a simple way your **best self** would address these toxic creator beliefs.

____

____

____

Chapter 3

You Are NOT an Imposter

This is a major problem.

I'm not gonna lie, I hate even having to address the concept of imposter syndrome because I believe, to some extent, it's bogus. And we'll touch on that later in this chapter, but it is something people have challenges with.

So, let's discredit the devil again.

What is Imposter Syndrome?

There are many definitions of this, but here are some of the most common I encounter when working with creators.

It is the belief that you, by nature of pursuing your goals, are an imposter.

That you're *pretending* to be some expert, some coach in your niche, and that one day you will be found out, exposed, and shown for the imposter that you are.

Imagine being a pilot of a commercial aircraft, and you're all dressed up allowing people to board the plane, wearing the pilot's hat, and making the announcements of the weather before takeoff, flight time, and maybe even the occasional corny joke to put the guests at ease.

But, and a really big but, you have NO CLUE about the first thing about being a pilot. You're just pretending to be one!

THIS is an imposter!

This is an example of someone who has no business being behind the wheel and in the pilot's chair.

However, that's not you.

You've done some level of work to put in the time to share your content online, have some sort of experience and expertise in what you do that debunks this whole theory and concept of being an imposter.

There's nothing to expose. You are who you say you are.

Why I Believe Imposter Syndrome Is Bogus

Consider this: you actually have some experience in what you're doing, even if you've only been putting in practice hours and training.

What many new video creators struggle with is calling, addressing, and accepting themselves as [insert your niche's professional title].

Those limiting beliefs we addressed in chapter one begin to show their ugly little heads, and you add to them by saying:

"I'm not good enough."

"I'm not as good as {insert another video creator's name}."

"I don't have the time to create video content."

"I don't have a team, and I'm too busy to do it myself."

All of these are, say it with me, **excuses**.

Remember, **all excuses are equal**.

One of the greatest quotes I was made to recite when I first attended college at the great Alabama A&M University, The Marching Maroon & White Band (Go Bulldogs!), was a quote about excuses.

> *"Excuses are tools of the incompetent which build monuments of nothingness, and those who indulge seldom accomplish anything at all."*

This is something I recite by heart and is branded in my memory that I love to couple with the scripture.

> "God did not give me the spirit of fear but of power, love and of a sound mind." ~ 2 Timothy 1:7

We all have fears.

It's part of the condition known as being human, but we also have the power to control how we feel by governing how and what we think. You *will* have what you say.

Have you somehow arrived to where you are by accident or mistake? Should there be someone "better" fulfilling your role?

I think not.

You've worked so very hard to be where you are. When presented with opportunities, realize that you've worked for them.

I can remember at several major stages of accomplishing a goal I had, I would sometimes think "why me" on a day.

There's a blessing in the statement a friend once shared with me that I will never forget saying, "You are created for such a time as this."

I had just shared publicly about achieving and hitting a goal I had long desired to achieve and he said it in a state of amazement and confirmation.

In moments when I would have weaker states of mind or simply battle depression around major life changes, I would often repeat to myself, "I was created for such a time as this. I am operating in my purpose and I am the right person to share what I've been created to. I'm built for this."

I would profess that over and over along with, "God did not give me the spirit of fear and with Him there is no lack."

Weak states of mind are bound to appear.

I highly recommend crafting an affirming statement that you can repeat over and over and over again. So, when the day comes and you find yourself wondering if you are good enough, speak life into what the real truth is.

Will you do some things in your business or set certain goals you sometimes feel are ridiculous? Absolutely.

But if it were not something you could do or actually desired, that goal would never have been documented and written on your heart. And, in the midst of moments you may find you can't seem to reaffirm the truth to yourself, be in community with life-giving friends and colleagues. Trust me, it makes a world of difference.

If you keep saying to yourself that you're not good enough and that you'll never make it and any other limiting belief you can think about, your subconscious mind will have no choice but to believe you.

The subconscious mind has one job, to say *yes*.

Have you ever found yourself walking down the street or in a building while being lost in thought when, suddenly, cutting through the noise of everything, your mind, body, and attention snap to focus when someone calls your name?

Your body and your mind are used to responding to your name over any other name on the planet. From the time of birth, we're trained to respond to our name and no other.

Your belief systems operate the same way.

You tell yourself something long enough and consistently enough, and your subconscious mind will agree with you and do all that's within its power to say,

"Sure, Diana, I'll believe that for you, and do everything I can to maintain that statement as fact and truth."

If you don't believe in the power of what you say, you might as well close this book and call it a day because you'll give up your ability to create change in your life when you don't recognize the power you have.

However, if you ***do*** believe you were created for a reason and that you have a unique purpose only you can fulfill, keep reading.

The Shark and The Goldfish

Some of the greatest lessons I learned in life came from spending time with my favorite aunt. She refused to accept the limiting beliefs that I'd profess daily and defended trying to convince her "this is just the way that I am" as a young adult.

However, my aunt wouldn't accept that at all.

I was a *very* rough diamond in my college days, and she reached through all the pain and limiting beliefs I believed to be true about myself to reach me in one of the few ways anyone could back then, through books.

I've always adored reading books, but never as much as when I lived in Ohio when a local college professor of mine, an overly excited history teacher, reinvigorated my love of learning, history, and reading.

Soon, I became an obsessive reader and learner, mostly of historical fiction and psychology self-help books, determined to find joy and meaning in my life, which I always believed was possible by unlocking the power of my mind and later my belief systems.

When my aunt saw how quickly I'd devour an 800-page book in a few days and wander off to the bookstore or my favorite thrift stores and book fairs to find new or gently used books, she started giving me these weekly reading assignments.

Every week, she tasked me with reading a new book on top of my full-time collegiate workload, and tell me I'd better have it read by the time she was ready to take me on some mandatory weekend errands with her where she'd ask me nonstop questions about the book she'd given me to study.

And boy, did I have an attitude back then because these were early-morning drives that lasted *all day*, and I wasn't keen on leaving the house.

I can't imagine how much work I was for her, because if I was anything, it was stubborn and negative as all hell. However, I'm grateful my aunt never gave up on me. She changed my life.

It's in reading these assigned books she'd given me and forcing me to share what I'd learned weekly that eventually landed me on a book called *The Shark and the Goldfish* by Jon Gordon.

This book is an incredible but short novel that tells the story of, you guessed it, a shark and a goldfish.

One day, a pet goldfish finds himself no longer in the comfort of his bowl but exposed to the great sea when a family day at the beach turns into a disaster with the goldfish being swept away into the ocean.

The goldfish is terrified and now exposed to the expanse of the ocean, and because it's the end of the day, he's left wondering what most of us ask ourselves daily.

"What am I going to eat for dinner?"

There's one unique difference between the behaviors, thought processes, and expectations of sharks and goldfish:

- Goldfish wait to be fed; Sharks hunt to eat.

It's in this unlikely friendship between this poor lost goldfish and seasoned great white shark that, instead of becoming another beach casualty, this goldfish learns to fend for himself and begins to *think* like a shark.

Right now, you're the goldfish.

You're used to being comfortably nestled in your bowl of business, which is the comfortable environment where you are a pro.

Video and YouTube Content Creation is your new ocean, and you don't know how to hunt and take care of yourself.

That is, until you picked up this book.

Now, let's transform you from a goldfish to a shark.

Let's hunt!

CREATOR NEXT STEPS

- [ ] Write out your statement of faith to encourage yourself when battling moments of weak states of mind.

____

____

____

____

____

Phase 2 | Maximizing Your Time to Create Engaging Videos

Chapter 4

Creating at Less Than 100%

I never planned for this.

I had just moved into my new apartment after moving back to St. Louis, and within a couple of months, I'd soon uncover life was about to become very different.

At the time I'm writing this book, some 61 million adult Americans suffer from some form of disability.[2] So, it goes without saying, you could throw a rock outside and it'd likely land on somebody that has some ailment they're suffering from or know someone with one.

While I hope that's not the case for you, dear reader, but the probability is still fair that you or someone you know has some chronic illness, disability, or challenge that keeps them from being able to operate at 100% at all times. I would like to say this sucks, but what I've uncovered in the last seven years of living with a chronic illness has made me more creative and a much stronger-willed person than I was before when I felt like I always had "more time" and was just getting to the prime of my life.

If you find yourself in a similar case, you're in luck!

You just so happened to pick up the right book that's going to show you how you can overcome that by working with your life challenge and your time constraints and come out the other side a conqueror. If you're one of those that don't battle any health challenges, you'll learn how to use your existing time constraints to become an even more efficient content-creating entrepreneur.

Constraints are just containers.

The legendary Stan Lee will forever hold my gratitude because he took the unique perspective to create a league of characters with disabilities and physical challenges and turn them into literal superheroes. On that note, Storm is better than Jean Grey–it's a fact. Jean Grey was lazy but moving right along.

If I can tap into a fraction of that creativity, this phase in the book on time will help you learn to work within your constraints versus be limited by them.

It begins with learning to see your time differently.

Leveraging Your Constraints

Suffering from a chronic disease, working a full-time job, and learning YouTube and content creation on the side meant I needed to learn to develop a system that could leverage the days I didn't feel well and those I did, which was always random.

Instead of focusing on what I couldn't do, I needed to refocus on what I *could* do. Once I did this, it became a system I still use to this day that will help you no matter if you suffer any health challenges or not.

The simple solution was to plan when I was unwell and create when I was.

Granted, there are some days when I just couldn't seem to "get a day off" and had to push through the pain and discomfort to create content. Only you can be the judge of when you can push through and when you need to take a break. So, use your best judgment proceeding with what I'm about to share with you.

To create effectively, the content has to first be planned and ready for recording.

Delaying until a day when you're feeling great can sometimes make you feel like you've wasted the day or rushed to create content unsure of when you'll feel well again. (Don't worry, there's a system I use for that as well to create, edit, and upload in a single day I'll share with you as well.)

Capturing Your Content

Depending on how busy or well you may feel from one day to another, the goal is to work within your constraints versus being limited by them.

As ideas have the fun habit of popping into your head at the weirdest times, the number one priority is capturing it. Losing great ideas can really hurt your feelings when you just *know* it was great and can't remember it for the life of you. We're going to avoid that all too-common unpleasantness.

Use a note system like Apple Notes or Google Notes that will sync across multiple devices and you can insert audio notes along with written notes and images.

I recommend these basic simple notes systems instead of other popular notes apps because we need to remove as many barriers as possible when creating. As app programmers have a goal of making the app better and better, sometimes too many options can lead you into analysis paralysis.

That's not what's needed here.

Use whatever you're already comfortable with, but if you're not using any notes app system at all, start with Apple Notes, Google Notes, or Notion.so.

Create the following three folders:

1. Capture
2. In Progress
3. Done/Recorded

When you're busy or feeling unwell, the number one priority is to capture your video ideas. This doesn't need to be pretty; it just needs to be efficient.

There are three main ways you want to be able to capture your ideas:

- Audio Notes
- Written Notes
- Taking Image-Based Notes

Capturing Your Ideas

Most note apps allow you to add audio notes to the note you're working on. However, add your native voice recorder or voice memos app already built into your phone to your phone's home page.

That way, no matter what, you can always start the voice memo app and record your ideas and add them to your notes later. You can also ask Siri or the Google Assistant and trigger your digital voice assistant to take a note or start the voice memo app for you.

This comes in handy, especially on those days you're not operating at 100% or have a brilliant idea while driving and never have to physically touch your phone to capture your idea.

Beginning to Plan Your Videos

The "In-Progress" section of your notes apps is when you've had the time to start planning out your video idea and move your video idea from **Capture** to **In Progress**.

Within your In-Progress folder, create a sub-folder called "Ready to Record," so as you finish planning out a video idea, you know which videos are completely ready for you to record.

I like to use emoji numbers to show the numbered order I want to record my videos in. As you plan out more and more videos, you'll want to prioritize those you want to record on your next planned recording date.

If you find you have a lot of videos in your In-Progress folder, pin those ideas you want to record next to the top so they don't get buried among your other video ideas.

The great thing about these three content folders to help manage your ideas is that you can easily move video ideas from one folder to the next. There are times I'll start planning a video and realize that a particular idea needs to wait. When I have to prioritize something else, I can easily add it back to the Capture folder.

While working and planning a video idea, keep it in the In-Progress folder. Once the video idea is completely ready to record, add it to the **Ready to Record** sub-folder.

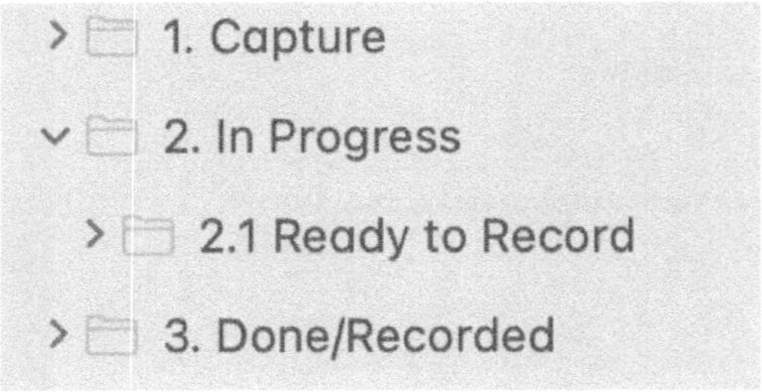

After You've Recorded Your Video

Once you've recorded your video, you can move it to the **"Done"** folder.

You can delete this note, but I find it helpful to hold on to the note until the video is published.

The finished notes are a great handoff to my video editor to see the video's written outline and for me to reference when working on new video ideas to quickly revisit noted ideas from previous videos.

This simple system has allowed me to process literally hundreds of video ideas from podcast episodes, micro-content ideas, and regular YouTube video content.

However, without a system to identify how long a video will take me to record, this system remains incomplete without the next chapter, where we dive into the Content Quadrant.

CREATOR NEXT STEPS

- [ ] Create your cross-device content structure to track your new video content ideas.
- [ ] Create sub-folders for your primary content that you'll distribute online: YouTube videos, video podcast, live streams, etc.

RESOURCES

- Apple Notes
- Google Notes
- Download 50+ video ideas worksheet here: OneRightVideo.com/VideoIdeas

Chapter 5

The Key to Not Wasting Time When Creating & Recording Videos

Nothing's worse than wasted time.

When you're unsure of how long a video will take you to record and you estimate incorrectly, you run into the uncomfortable position of not recording, assuming it'll take too much time, or get flustered rushing, trying to do "#everything" in the allotted time.

Creating video content does not have to be an all-day event, even if you're brand new to creating video content.

Once you learn to properly segment your content creation time, you'll learn to leverage your time constraints instead of cursing them.

The Content Quadrant

One thing that constantly plagues many entrepreneurs is that we're busy.

Outside of being an entrepreneur, we have families, friends, and hopefully, a social life of some sort, among other things that command our time already. Adding on video content creation can be stressful and annoying without the right system of efficiencies to help make creating videos easier.

The **Content Quadrant** is a system I created and still use to this day to make sure no matter how much time I have, I can plan my videos according to my schedule without feeling rushed or stressed about what video I have time to create and how long it would take to record.

The four sections of the Content Quadrant are:

➢ **Quadrant 1:** Quick Hitters

➢ **Quadrant 2:** Light Planners

➢ **Quadrant 3:** Medium Planners

➢ **Quadrant 4:** Hard Hitters

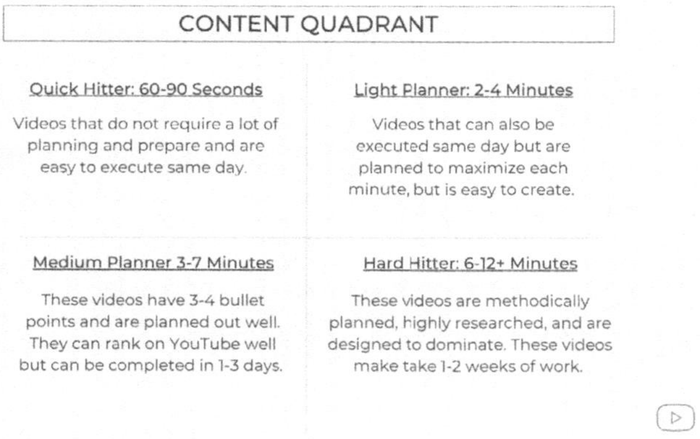

Each quadrant is based on the estimated length of the raw video file and how long the final video should be once edited.

The timeframes for each section are rough estimates of how long the finished video should be versus how long it'll take to record the video.

Creating a running list of videos easily becomes an organized list broken down into sections when you leverage the Content Quadrant.

With a goal set to begin with the end in mind, you can look at your regular work and life schedule, identify what time slots you have available to create your videos, and easily sort through the video ideas within that content quadrant.

Before recording solely based on the Content Quadrant, first set the expectation of how long the video should be.

In Phase 4 Video Content Creation, we'll cover how to properly plan a video, but for now, we're going to handle your time constraints and see what video you actually have time to create first.

Quadrant 1 | Quick Hitters (60-90 Seconds)

Quick Hitters are 60-90 second long videos that do not require a lot of planning or preparation and are easy to execute the same day you're recording.

This could be a TikTok, YouTube Shorts or Instagram Reel video, a promotional video, a series of IG or YouTube Stories where you're leveraging a trending sound, dance, etc.

Quick Hitters are fun to make because they don't take a lot of time to create. They're easy to record, edit, and upload—less than 15 minutes if editing is required. Many of these content forms can be created directly inside the corresponding app with the built-in app tools.

Even though Quick Hitters don't require a lot of time to execute, you can still plan these videos out.

You can save the trending sound link to your notes application when normally watching or consuming content you enjoy, what ideas you had to use with that trending sound, what point you want to cover in the YouTube Short, etc.

These styles of videos are highly shareable, easy, and quick to record.

Ten to fifteen minutes doesn't seem like a lot of time to do much of anything, but when you have ideas already categorized using the Content Quadrant, the 10-15 minutes you might waste looking for an idea is instead invested in recording the idea you already captured.

I've loved using open 15-minute segments of time in my schedule to record and edit several Quick Hitters or even fun skits that include multiple characters.

There may be times when your schedule is full and you're desiring to take some portion of the day to create content.

Quick Hitters are a great option.

Quadrant 2 | Light Planners (2-4 Minutes)

Light Planners are two to four-minute videos that can also be executed on the same day.

These can be easy and simple tutorials or informational videos that don't require a lot of prior planning.

This style of video is as the name implies; requires light planning in order to execute. These are my secret weapons when I need to record, edit, and upload a video in a single day.

A Light Planner could be

- an updated video of a new feature your company is introducing or on tools/services you use in your business
- a short tutorial or an informational video answering a commonly asked question from your audience
- or, it could be a highly searched-for question that simply doesn't require a longer video to address the issue fully.

Despite being a shorter video, you can still implement a normal video recording structure to create it.

These are still highly valuable videos and can do very well on YouTube because they're short and straight to the point.

The estimated recording time for these still falls within the 10-15 minute recording window to create. This isn't a rushed 15-minute window, but one you can, over time, record two Light Planners with little to no re-recorded segments.

Remember, you know your content and you're skilled in what you're discussing.

Don't think you can do this? Here are some video ideas that would be great for Light Planners:

- **The #1 Mistake New {insert profession, type of person, etc.} Make When {insert action}**
    - Example: The #1 Mistake New Fiction Writers Make When Writing Their First Book

- **One Thing Every {blank} Gets Wrong About {insert process/profession, etc.}**
    - Every 1st Time Home Owner Gets This ONE THING Wrong on Their Loan Application

Quadrant 3 | Medium Planners (3-7 Minutes)

Medium Planners are usually a content-creating entrepreneur's bread and butter.

These videos can range from three to seven minutes but are highly researched and well-planned videos. Just because they're not 10- and 12-minute videos, doesn't mean you can't have a well-executed piece of content your audience loves and will binge-watch.

These could be your primary pieces of content where you're giving an in-depth analysis of some area in your business. They differ from Light Planners because these are videos you may intend to rank on YouTube because they're highly searched queries in your niche. When working with videos like these, it may take longer to record because you're being very intentional about how you deliver your content and the review process may take longer.

For a Medium Planner, I like to have at least 20 minutes set aside for recording time to make sure I can have space to re-record certain segments or plan for different segments in a video.

For example, one portion of a video might be recorded on my settee and the other half on the computer or repositioned to record the camera screen for certain parts of a tutorial.

When you have multiple location recordings, record everything you need in that position first before relocating.

If I have a set of seven videos I intend to record, I will record everything I need to while at my desk first. Then, if any parts require me to change the setup to record my camera screen, for example, I'll record all those segments in that area before proceeding.

This is even handier when recording videos outside of your home or office.

Recording everything one particular video requires and all the various locations, finishing, and then possibly repeating that again for another video can be tiring. Not truly physically tiring, but it can introduce a type of creative exhaustion and a lot of downtimes in between recordings, which is very inefficient.

Quadrant 4 | Hard Hitters (6-12+ Minutes)

Hard Hitters range from six to twelve minutes or longer. Not to be confused with Medium Planners because of the overlapping timeframes, Hard Hitters require a bit more work and research.

The estimated recording timeframe is still within 20-30 minutes to record, similar to Medium Planners, but the additional time and work into the video is increased based on the research required to complete and can play into how long it may take this video to be edited to completion.

These are great, in-depth videos that are highly researched, well thought out, and planned.

These can be your longer 15- and 20-minute full-length tutorials, podcasts, or training videos in your niche. These could even be snippets from your video podcast, interview, or talk that you've repurposed into a video for your channel.

A Hard Hitter isn't categorized as such solely based on time, but because of the complexity that might be needed for producing the video. Other elements to factor into the various quadrants also include how long it takes to transition the video concept from idea to being uploaded on YouTube.

I did something fun in a video where the real-time editing version of myself (the future me) interacted with the recorded version of myself (still recording the video on the screen) and the two versions of myself had a quick dialogue.

In film, this is called breaking the third wall. It's when you see a character look at you and break character while still in the video scene acting.

Introducing this layer of complexity is surprisingly very simple to do but may require recording a few takes to make sure I could nail it in one sitting and get the timing correct.

Granted, this isn't your traditional tutorial video, but it's great to introduce elements of your personality or fresh ideas to create something fun and different.

Another example of a Hard Hitter is my camera walkthrough videos, which may take a full 20-30 minutes to record every menu and optimize the camera for video recording.

Categorizing Your Videos

The Content Quadrant is a great and effective way to categorize your video ideas for the busy content-creating entrepreneur because it allows you to review your calendar and easily identify blocks of time you can dedicate to recording content.

If you know you only have 15 minutes to record a video in a busy week, you can easily squeeze in a Quick Hitter or Light Planner to best use that time.

If you know you need to cover an in-depth topic, time block space to record a Hard Hitter so you have plenty of time to cover all the necessary areas without rushing through the content because you're busy.

The more videos you create, the better you become at estimating how long it will take you to create various video types.

No matter how busy you are, you can always leverage the Content Quadrant to schedule accurate blocks of time to create videos that serve your audience and help build your brand.

The next step in being able to record your video content more efficiently is setting up your recording space to take virtually no time to record, even edit, and upload a video in a single day.

CREATOR NEXT STEPS

- [ ] Categorize your existing video ideas based on the Content Quadrant.

RESOURCES

- Download the Video Planning Guide here: OneRightVideo.com/VideoPlanningGuide

Phase 3 | Camera Gear & Technology Simplified

Chapter 6

Creating a Pro-Level Video Creation Studio

I've answered the question, "What gear do I need to get started on YouTube?" more times than I can count. And yet I'm grateful for every time I can answer that question for someone beginning their creative journey to share this single piece of advice:

- Invest in a **system of gear** versus spot-buying individual gear without a plan.

However, that's not where most creators find themselves when investing in gear. It first starts with a camera, not necessary accessories like a memory card, lighting, or audio equipment, and a long process of finding things out slowly and expensively.

Whether you've bought a few pieces of gear or are just getting started building a studio in this chapter, I'll break down for you:

- what the basic needs of a content-creating entrepreneur's studio should consist of

- what to buy
- and in what order to buy to avoid wasting your time, energy, and money.

Creating a List of Non-Negotiables

We're beyond the days when the go-to camera recommendation would be a DSLR camera, and we're now into the era of super-powerful mirrorless cameras.

They're faster, more efficient, higher quality, and a great companion to creators of all types. Once you've gotten your belief system onboard to serve you in your content creation journey, you can move on to the fun stuff: buying gear.

When you're looking to invest in a camera, you need to **develop your list of non-negotiables**.

This is a list of your bare bones, must-have features in a camera that are going to solve problems instead of creating them due to the limitations of the equipment. Not sure what you'll need or what a camera should have?

Here's a list of must-have baseline features I believe every camera should have when getting started in video:

— Accurate and Reliable Face Detection Autofocus

— 4k Video Recording

— Unlimited Video Recording Times

— Image Stabilization: Digital and/or In-Body Image Stabilization (IBIS)

— Microphone Input Port

— Headphone Input Port

— Clean HDMI Out Signal (for live streaming)

— Flip-Out Screen/Fully Articulating Screen

— Great Lens Options to Choose From

This is the list of what I call your non-negotiables.

The more you create, the more you may uncover additional camera features available in newer camera models that increase your efficiency and/or creativity.

A great example of this is when the camera brand Sony created a feature called Product Showcase mode in video mode. This introduced a solution for creators needing to regularly show items to the camera and needing to repeatedly block their face to temporarily get the camera to focus on the item.

Product Showcase mode solved this problem and sped up the creative workflow and efficiency when recording by not having to pause and constantly wait for the camera to acquire focus and focus on the item, adding more areas needing correction when editing.

While not an absolute must-have for all creators, you can see how simple new features can improve how you create.

You want a camera whose features create a high enough ceiling that the camera truly operates as an efficient tool and any limitations don't disrupt your creative workflow.

When It's Wise to Upgrade Your Gear

There are three primary reasons when it makes sense to upgrade any gear you invest in:

1. When it will increase your creative abilities and efficiency with new features or models.

2. When the upgrade will solve a problem you regularly encounter when creating or will soon.

3. If you solely want the new gear.

Instead of going in order from items one through three, I want to tackle the third option quickly.

It should go without saying, but as an adult, if you want something, get it. Far too often, I find content-creating entrepreneurs desiring to get something new and coming up with wild reasons to justify the purchase.

If you just want the item you're eyeing, you don't need a logical reason to want it.

However, if your goal is to invest wisely and avoid going too deep into the weeds, get what you need and get to work using it. As you identify new areas that could be improved based on how you create, invest up.

A great example of this is the coach/speaker/trainer-style creator needing to record their talks but only owning a camera that records in 30-minute increments before shutting off.

For the content marketing-driven creator, this is an instant reason to upgrade your camera because you've identified a limitation that will impact the efficiency of how you create.

Recording your talk, only to review the footage and see part of your presentation was cut out, and any Q&A segment is completely missing is frustrating. That's why any cameras I recommend must first meet that list of non-negotiables where unlimited recording is a must-have.

Two Warnings Before You Buy

1. Tech's Lifespan is Short

When you're going down the rabbit hole of researching gear online, you'll quickly run into what's called "evergreen content."

The beauty and curse of YouTube is that when you search for something, you'll find videos that were created that week, alongside videos created three years ago or longer. And three years old in the tech space is a *long* time.

When researching what gear to buy, and you begin to compare one camera versus another, watch out for videos that are over three years old.

It doesn't mean what you're considering is bad or not worth investing in, but it can mean that likely a newer improved model may be available, or on the brink of being announced.

2. Compare Gear Based on Your List of Non-Negotiables & Identify Its Limitations

All gear looks perfect online.

While the dopamine hits of excitement are surging through your veins, and the urge to hit "Add to Cart" kicks in, it's easy to overlook what's on your list of non-negotiables.

So, before you check out, just double-check that the gear you're considering actually can do all of what you need it to do based on your list of non-negotiables and intended use case.

For a simple way to keep up with the ever-changing technology in the camera space, I developed a free camera quiz. It'll help you identify the best camera for video based on your intended use case that's regularly updated so that you never have to hunt for "*the best camera for...*" again.

You can access the camera quiz here: OneRightVideo.com/CameraQuiz

What Should You Include in Your Content Creation Studio?

Outside of identifying your list of non-negotiables for your camera, there are other elements to building out a competent and effective studio.

The hierarchy of needs is best broken down into a system I call A.L.V.A.S.

You may already be familiar with the basic camera needs of a camera, a microphone, and some lighting.

This is where most creators make the mistake and focus only on these three areas (often out of order) when purchasing new gear and equipment for video content creation.

If you're only focusing on audio, video, and lighting, no less in that order, which isn't accurate for investing wisely, you're more likely to make a series of investments that don't complement one another and/or over-invest in gear you really don't need but bought just because you saw it was heavily recommended on YouTube.

It's time you met Alvas!

A.L.V.A.S. is an acronym that stands for:

Audio

Lighting

Video

Accessories

and **S**oftware.

Remember, in algebra class, they taught you the acronym P.E.M.D.A.S., which stood for ***Please Excuse My Dear Aunt Sally,*** which really stood for remembering the proper order to complete equations in algebra:

— **P**arentheses

— **E**xponents

— **M**ultiplication

— **D**ivision

— **A**ddition

— and **S**ubtraction

If you're thinking to yourself that just hearing about mathematical equations stresses you out, you're not alone. That's as far as we're going with it.

Hearing about math would always trigger a memory for me of when I sat in my third-grade teacher's class in elementary school and we were supposed to learn our multiplication tables up to 12.

Of course, like any other kid, I played all summer long and waited until the last week of summer to pull out my perfectly crisp multiplication chart and try to rush learning them.

Needless to say, I failed.

I'd sit in her class with my heart pounding as she'd tell us to pull out our math books, and start handing out worksheets.

I wore down that cheat sheet of all the answers so badly that my mother hand-wrote them out on a yellow pad of paper inside a clear paper protector and stapled it so I could have a reference sheet anytime I needed it that wouldn't wear down.

As long as I had this sheet, I felt confident and bulletproof whenever it was time to switch to math in school.

Until one day, the teacher got hip to my yellow reference sheet and told me to put it inside my desk and learn my "times tables," as they were called, by heart.

I was crushed.

Just like that, my confidence disappeared and only got worse during tests because I couldn't recall them by heart.

The A.L.V.A.S. Hierarchy of Investments gives you an order to easily remember when making purchases to build a content creation studio so that you're buying equipment that complements and actually is compatible with other components in your studio instead of spot-buying items that overlap and send you into creative constipation.

To avoid your eyes glazing over because the next couple of chapters are technical chapters, we're going to keep this simple.

While some elements are easily explained via video, that you can watch in the course that accompanies this book, you can always find the most up-to-date information on my YouTube channel here: OneRightVideo.com/YouTube

CREATOR NEXT STEPS

- [ ] Create a list of non-negotiables to list features your camera should have that will make content creation easier for you.
- [ ] Write down all the current gear your have to create content and where it fits in the A.LV.A.S. Hierarchy of Investments.

Chapter 7

Audio is Greater Than Video

Have you ever watched a video on YouTube where there's a constant whooshing loud sound, cutting out their words and making it difficult to hear because the wind is blowing too hard?

How likely are you to click away from that video or skip ahead to see if the audio is better later on in the video?

People will forgive poor video quality, but they are not likely to keep watching your videos if the audio is poor. Your audio is far greater than the quality of your video. That's why "A" in the A.L.V.A.S. Hierarchy of Investing for audio is first.

Audio needs for video creators are broken down into 3 key areas:

1. Learning to Read the Room

2. Reducing Noise in Your Recording Space

3. Investing in Microphones Based on the Intended Use Case

1. Learning to Read the Room

To get consistently great audio, the first thing you want to do is invest in audio gear **based on your environment.**

Whether you're working in your home office, the corner of your living room or a dedicated space in your den or basement, stand at the entrance of where you plan to record. What do you see and hear?

- When you close your eyes, what do you hear in that space? Is it loud or relatively quiet?

Here's a list of audible disturbances to consider and watch out for:

— furnaces or air-conditioning unit

— loud footsteps or nearby room/house activity

— refrigerators

— large echoes created from being in a large room

— washing machines

— kids' playroom or den

This sounds like overkill, but if you make the mistake of just picking a place to record and only search on YouTube to see what the most recommended microphone is, that's a great way to waste your money.

You want to invest in audio solutions based on the space you're recording in 80%-90% of the time and the type of content you'll be creating.

It's not until you create videos that you notice these small things that otherwise you'd mentally tune out. While some noises can be greatly reduced or completely omitted in editing, not all noises can be removed when they're simply too loud and happening while you're actively speaking in a video.

2. Reducing Noise In Your Recording Space

If you're like me, you may have a typical home office you're not keen to redecorate to the atypical "video gamer's den look" with triangular-shaped foam pads all over the walls for reducing noises while recording videos.

Sounds panels are a great investment to reduce the noise in your space and offer very tasteful design options that would suit any styled office.

A simple Amazon or Google search for "acoustic panels" can yield some options that easily blend with any decor style, and even those designed with images to appear as a canvas painting only; There are known as "art acoustic panels."

Positioning these panels properly so they capture the audio reflections bouncing on the walls takes a bit of know-how and can be done one of two ways:

1. A DIY approach coupled with a YouTube how-to search.
2. Hire a company to Assess Your Space and do it for you.

Depending on the size of the panels needed, and how large of a space you'll be covering, the expenses for doing this can vary from a couple of hundred dollars to a couple of thousand dollars for large spaces.

Taking the DIY approach, placing an area rug, sound panels, or even sound blankets over windows, softer desk mats, and having some plush textures or surfaces in a room can drastically change the sound in a space.

3. Investing in Microphones Based on Your Intended Use Case

There are three primary microphone types that serve content-creating entrepreneurs best.

These are microphone options that will help limit background noises, be versatile enough that you can use them when recording your talks and presentations, and microphones great for everyday use in meetings and of course your YouTube videos.

The three primary microphone types you should have in your creative arsenal are:

1. Podcast-Style Microphones
2. Lapel Styled Microphones (with or without a wireless unit)
3. Vlogging/Shotgun-Style Microphones

There's a myriad of microphone options on the market to choose from and each comes with its own set of features and limitations.

Unlike choosing a camera, selecting a microphone is much easier because audio is very forgiving and flexible. The key is to build an audio setup that serves you versus stresses you out.

Mic Type #1: Podcast-Style Microphones

This is a must-have microphone because it's not just for creating content but when speaking on client calls, speaking at virtual events, and more.

There are many different styles of microphones, but I believe cardioid-dynamic podcast-style microphones are best for content-creating entrepreneurs. This is not only my personal favorite but what roughly 95% of my clients use when recording content in their home office or studio setups.

These microphones are perfect for rejecting background noise and only picking up audio from in front of the microphone, only extending out to around about the size of your head.

A great benefit of a podcast-style mic is that you set it up once and don't have to change or update it unless you choose to.

Unless the background noise is extremely loud, like a jet or airplane flying over your home, you're likely not going to hear normal ambient home noises like your furnace or air conditioner, children playing in the next room, and so forth.

XLR vs. USB Microphones

There are two primary microphone connection types you'll encounter the most on podcast-style microphones, and that's USB microphones or XLR microphones.

USB microphones are usually one of two styles: either a USB-C port style or a USB Micro or Mini style. Because the style can vary from mic to mic, most brands include an array of cables and connections to make sure they can connect to your devices easily.

If you're just getting started, and you're not looking to get into the weeds selecting a good microphone—you just want it to work and make sure you sound awesome—go with a USB microphone. More specifically, go with a hybrid-style microphone like the Shure MV7.

This microphone can connect directly to your computer and is extremely user-friendly. It even includes some user-friendly software to help give you that radio-quality sound, even though it may be your first day using it and you know nothing about microphones.

XLR microphones have ports that are the more traditional analog audio ports in the shape of a circle with three prongs within that circle. Any microphones you've typically seen at a music concert, church, or just about any small event was likely an XLR-connected microphone.

The more industry-standard and high-quality microphones are almost always XLR-only microphones, like the legendary Shure SM7B that icons like Quincy Jones and Michael Jackson have used. They can range from budget-friendly options like another legendary microphone, the Shure SM58, or higher-end microphones like the Heil PR-40 or Shure SM7B.

XLR microphones benefit from having what's called a low-noise floor. This means when no one is speaking, the ambient audio that's usually picked up from the room itself, it's very quiet. However, XLR microphones require what's called an audio interface to connect to your computer or smartphone.

The goal with your audio is for the viewer not to notice any audibly distracting noises in the background.

Mic Type #2: Wired Lapel Microphones w/ Wireless Units

A simple lapel microphone will always be one of the most versatile microphone types all creators have in their arsenal of gear.

These are the small microphones you'll commonly see clipped to creators, newscasters, or interviewers' shirts that provide a simple and clear way to pick up audio from the person speaking.

You can buy most lapel microphones in a creator bundle or kit of some sort, with everything you'd need in the kit. This allows you to connect directly to your camera or use a wireless unit to keep you untethered from your camera.

A great go-to option is the Rode Wireless Go 2 with the Rode Go lapel microphone set.

This allows you to record your talks on stages and still have your audio connected to your microphone while giving you the freedom to be untethered from your camera source.

Should You Record Your Audio Separately From Your Videos?

You may be thinking,

"But, Diana, what about just recording separately and syncing the audio afterward?"

I have a very simple response to that: No.

You can, but what purpose would that serve the already busy and time-conscious entrepreneur?

While there are some of us entrepreneur content creators that love the gear and tech side of things, most do not. I can appreciate that even for the tech-loving creator investing unnecessary time in majoring in the minor is still a poor use of time. Unless there's a specific and logical reason to do so, don't.

This is not my cup of tea or even something I would recommend doing for 95% of entrepreneurs unless you're experienced with editing and working with your gear.

You'll often hear this recommendation from indie filmmakers, audio technicians, or folks that eat, sleep, and dream about audio – I'm not one of those people, and you don't need to be either.

The reason I recommend kits like the Rode Wireless Go 2 is because it includes internal audio recording, in addition to wirelessly connecting to your camera or smartphone. You can have both; the best of both worlds.

You don't need to choose; you can have both!

After previously speaking at a large industry-leading social media conference, I used the Rode Wireless Go 2 to connect to my camera to record my talk. The audio tech operating the room also used a Rode Wireless Go 2 to capture my audio for the live virtual attendees and for the recording of the event.

While doing my talk, I walked freely from one side of the stage to the other and met with an eager group of attendees after my session in the hall to answer more questions. Throughout the entire time, I never turned off my microphone, and I didn't have to worry about the audio.

Mic Type #3: On The Go Vlogging & Shotgun-Style Microphones

Before you possibly start cycling the ideas in your head of how you don't intend to vlog and don't want to, that's not the sole purpose of a vlog-style microphone.

While I believe vlogging is a powerful storytelling content element businesses should leverage in various ways, these style microphones serve a different purpose. Being untethered and not desiring to always clip a mic to your person, shotgun-style microphones are great for:

- Mounting to your camera when creating on-the-go; traveling, recording various areas in your office, etc.

- Positioning out of sight, to a fixed and mounted position where you record.

- Attached to a tripod or recording stand to move with the stand.

The versatility is the key benefit of these microphones. However, if you're recording in a larger room or a noisy environment, opting for a shotgun-style microphone that rejects a bit more noise is best.

There is what's called the microphone pickup pattern that determines how much audio is picked up or registered clearly versus what's rejected. The most common options targeted at content creators are either super-cardioid or omnidirectional.

The technical difference between how these two options work and how they'll impact you is minimizing environmental noises around you, like when recording at an event or when the furnace kicks on in your office while picking up the audio from your voice.

My Top Audio Recommendations

Now that you're more educated on your microphone options and how they can be useful to your content workflow, here are my top recommendations to invest in that serve you and your workflow:

<u>Beginner/Intermediate Audio Setups</u>

1. Podcast Style Setup

- Shure MV7 USB/XLR Microphone

2. Lapel Style Setup

- Rode Go Lapel Microphone w/ Rode Wireless Go 2 Wireless Microphone Kit

3. Shotgun Style Mic

- Movo VXR10 or Rode VideoMicro I & II

Pro-Level Audio Setup

1. Podcast Style Setup

- Rodecaster Pro 2 + Shure SM7B XLR Microphone

2. Lapel Style Setup

- Sony UWP-D Wireless System

3. Shotgun Style Mic

- Rode VideoMic NTG Hybrid Analog/USB Mic

The Gift and Curse of Budget-Friendly Gear

When you're looking to invest in pro-level equipment, the most expensive gear doesn't mean it's the best for you.

I always encourage my clients to invest in what will currently meet their needs, but also has a large enough ceiling in features to still be a viable option as their skills and content goals improve.

The problem with investing in gear that's only based on price vs its features and intended use case is that you'll end up like one of my clients, whom we'll call Noah.

Noah had the unique problem of asking what was always the cheapest, until finally, in about our second coaching call, I explained to Noah that if he insisted on only buying gear based on price, this wasn't going to work.

I understand everyone has some level of financial comfort or limit when investing in gear and equipment, but that he needed to put that aside and trust the recommendations I was giving him because they would best serve his right-now needs and future goals.

Noah took my advice on some things he felt comfortable with and on the larger purchases, like the Rodecaster Pro recommendation and specific camera recommendations, he instead selected based on price alone and went with cheaper options.

A couple of months went by after Noah and I finished working together on getting him set up with video and learning the basics when navigating YouTube, until one day, I received an email from him, and I could tell he was pissed!

The email was full of a bunch of "how do I do this" and "why can't my camera do X" questions until the email finally ended with,

"I'm just ready to sell all this crap because none of it's working like I see other people creating in their videos. I need your help!"

I knew this email would eventually come because it always does for those that like to be hard-headed, as my mother would say.

My email reply to Noah was simple.

"Noah, I can appreciate and empathize with where you're at and how frustrated you're feeling right now, trying to get everything to work, so you can create videos the way you envision to.

However, if you recall from our prior conversations during your coaching sessions, I warned you this was the likely result of the gear you ultimately chose to invest in.

The answer to all your questions is that your audio and camera setup cannot do what you're trying to do because of the limitations they have.

I can share with you a few ways to attempt some workarounds or hacks, but they aren't a reliable option I'd rely on long-term and ultimately will cost more than the proper gear to do the job.

You can invest in {insert list of the right gear I'd previously recommended} to solve all these issues and give you some additional flexibility in your workflow.

Let me know how you'd like to proceed."

After a couple of days, I assumed Noah was fed up enough not to reply, but I was pleasantly surprised when the email I received from him told me he not only ordered the gear I originally recommended but asked if based on his new content goals if that was still right for him or if he needed to get anything else.

Noah now creates content regularly on YouTube and is doing AWESOME! Anytime I pop in the chat of his live stream by surprise, I receive a warm hello and statements of gratitude for helping him get the right gear.

I understand investing in all this gear can start to add up and get pretty darn expensive.

However, when you've decided to become a content-creating entrepreneur, it comes with investments, and investments should yield a return. If you find you're struggling with investing in a piece of gear you know you need and will solve your problems vs something much cheaper and doesn't have what you need, remember this:

> *When you buy too cheaply, you also buy the problems that come with being cheap.* ~ Diana Gladney

CREATOR NEXT STEPS

- [ ] Make sure your gear list includes the three primary microphone types to maximize your creative flexibility.
- [ ] Write down all the current gear you use to create content and where it fits in the A.LV.A.S. Hierarchy of Investments.

Chapter 8

Properly Lighting Your Setup

My brand-new Canon T5i had finally arrived in the mail, and I felt O-Mazing!

It was one of the largest investments I had made in a long time, and I felt empowered to start creating videos! In my eyes, it was a high-class piece of tech versus an entry-level camera.

I unboxed my entire camera kit, set my camera up on a tripod, and went to sit down to record. It blew me away at the quality versus the "dumbphone" I was previously using.

The one thing I noticed was that the image was dark and looked dingy.

So, I got up and went to my computer and started researching in my university's video production research department for answers, YouTube. It was then that it finally registered for me that the recommendations for lights were far more important than I had realized.

Like many creators, I took the recommendation back then to use hardware store clamp lights and use daylight temperature light bulbs covered with printer paper or diffusion material to soften the lights. I walked into my local Lowe's and grabbed a pair of the eight-dollar clamp lights and walked home thinking "crisis averted"... until I turned the lights on.

The saying *looking like a deer in headlights* was exactly how I felt when I got home, clamped the lights on my office door and nearby bookshelf, trying to get my video to look like what I saw on YouTube.

The loud hum of the clamp lights, fear my printer paper covering the lights would catch fire, and eventual frustration finally made me invest in some good soft box lights that finally solved some of my lighting problems. Those I had from needing reliable lights for video, and to finally stop the annoying hum that was now in my videos, while I pretended not to look blinded as the deep dark shadows behind me danced around as I moved my hands, talking, creating my videos.

When done well, the right lighting can make a video look amazing, and while everyone asks "What camera are you using?", great video creators know your videos are only as good as your lighting.

The lights you select can either solve problems for you or create them. This is why your lights are the second priority in the A.L.V.A.S. Hierarchy of Investments.

Let's keep you from looking like a deer caught in headlights in your videos.

Lighting Tips for Beginners

Building Your Ideal Lighting Setup

When investing in a lighting kit, look around where you're going to record your videos.

Ask yourself:

— Do you have any ambient lighting sources like windows where you'll record?

— What time of day do you intend to record 90% of your videos?

— When your camera is in place, and you're sitting down to record, how much space do you have around you to place lights?

This is where a lot of new creators run into the problem of investing in a lighting setup that doesn't complement their current environment.

This is also where my good friend Jarrod found himself week after week, frustrated with his awesome-looking, yet non-functional, lighting setup.

One day, while on a call with Jarrod and our mutual friend Joshua, Jarrod finally announced how frustrated he was that he didn't have enough space with his existing lighting setup. It was a popular but rather large lighting setup with a softbox dome that was huge!

This conversation started soon after Josh recently redesigned his space and invested in a similar LED lighting kit that I use and recommend that has a much smaller footprint, yet is just as effective.

Especially since Jarrod was also working, like us, in a small spare bedroom converted to a home office and YouTube recording studio.

Jarrod was adamant about not getting any more gear and determined to make his lighting setup work, until he eventually got frustrated enough to cave in and get some LED light panels.

His lighting setup still looked excellent, but the amount of space he reclaimed from getting a smaller, space-friendly lighting setup to meet his needs made it easier for him to just come in the office and record without moving the light to sit down, and I would imagine feeling less claustrophobic with a UFO-shaped dome a hand's distance away.

Lighting Design Options for Your Videos

If you're ready to replace your existing lighting setup or make your first purchase in a lighting setup for video, you'll at least need two light sources with diffusion material to soften the light when it shines on your skin.

Your first lighting source will be your primary light source, known as your **key light**. Your second lighting source will be what's called your fill light.

Some creators prefer what's called Rembrandt lighting, where they predominantly use one key light source on one side of their face, creating a shadow on the other side of their face. They may also have, on the side or in the background, colored LED lights in the shot or what's known as practical lighting sources.

Practical lights are those you'll see like a house lamp in a creator's video, and it looks as if it's adding light to the person, when, in fact, the lamp is little more than decoration. There's a full light off to the side, actually providing the light source you think you're seeing in the video.

The lights you invest in should be based on your recording space, what existing light sources you have in that space, and the diffusion source to keep you from looking like a deer in headlights.

If your recording space has a window you'd like to use for video, you can use it as a primary or secondary lighting source.

Even with super bright window lighting in your recording space, you'll still need to have a light at the ready to provide consistent light.

Clouds passing over the sun, hiding it for a bit during the day, can impact the way your videos look. It won't be until you're editing your videos that you uncover things that weren't normal-looking and then, suddenly, everything looks very cool and has a blueish hue.

Troubleshooting Your Lighting Issues

Every week, I schedule time in my day to check my YouTube comments, among other social platforms, and one day, I saw a distressing comment from a lady, frustrated that her videos kept looking weird from one recording to the next, even though she recorded them all simultaneously.

I see these types of comments all the time when new video creators get frustrated with their cameras and gear when they're using the same equipment their favorite creators on YouTube are using, but their video looks nothing like what they see online.

This comes from not finding the devil in the small details and developing skills over time to become better.

When you're learning to light your videos, and you're trying to dial in a specific look, it sucks when you can't pinpoint why this keeps happening.

Let's walk through some common issues you might run into when you're learning to light your videos, so each of your videos looks the same even when they're recorded weeks or months apart.

Kelvins & Light Temperatures

One of the most common phrases you'll hear that pertains to lighting is the word "kelvins" or the lights' "temperature," which are the numbers used to measure your lights' white balance temperature.

This isn't temperature as in degrees, but a scale that goes from cool daylight temperature that tends to have a blueish or pure white hue and on the other side of the spectrum that has a warmer orange-type hue.

It's this lighting temperature scale that's known as kelvins.

If you've ever been to a hardware store and walked through their lighting department, you'll see a range of lights, but more importantly, different hues from different bulbs.

Some have a warmer hue that looks yellow to burnt orange and is great for living room environments. Other lights may have a daylight temperature and have a pure white and clean look. These are lights you may see in an office room and do not emit any type of warm hue.

When you're learning to light your videos and turn on your camera, if it's set to automatic, it's trying to decide what the image should look like based on the lighting in the space.

— Should it get brighter or darker?

— Should it assume the scenario should have a warm hue or a clean daylight temperature hue, or somewhere in the middle?

We don't want our camera making these decisions for us, so when you're adjusting the lights in your space, it's so that you can tell your camera what the lighting should look like so each video has a consistent look.

The Effects of Bad White Balance

Nearly all modern mirrorless cameras can set a custom white balance, so it doesn't change unless you manually do so.

If you're sitting down to record a video and notice it looks like you've joined the Blue Man Group or that you've turned into a Simpsons character, you're likely having a white balance issue that's throwing off your colors.

We easily resolve this by using what's called a Gray Card to allow the camera to capture a reading of what the light temperature is simply by you taking a picture.

Each camera does this a little differently, but it's super easy no matter what brand of camera you have.

When you hold up your gray card up to your camera and position it within this boxed frame to capture the room's light temperature, the camera takes a reading of the room and will adjust to the right lighting temperature so you don't have shifting color hues in your videos.

To see an example of this, I have a video tutorial on how to set this up on your camera that you can access by going here: OneRightVideo.com/whitebalance

My Top Lighting Recommendations for Video

It's very easy to find amazing lighting setups these days with excellent diffusion material to soften the harshness lights can give, and that's all you need: a good set of lights and diffusion material.

An easy all-in-one solution would be the lights I've used for years, which is the Viltrox VL-200 light set, complete with lighting stands, a wireless remote, and AC power chargers included, and a battery connection option built into each lamp for a wireless lighting setup. I couple this with The D-Fuse diffusion softbox set that easily fits over my LED panels to soften and diffuse the light.

There is such a wide array of amazing lighting setups that are available online, that it'd be virtually impossible to list them all. However, as with any type of electronics, there are more reliable brands and others that are questionable at best. Some brands you can trust include Viltrox, Aputure, GVM (Great Video Maker), Godox, and Amaran, among a few others. Even brands like SmallRig, Ulanzi, and Neewer create great continuous LED light solutions that are great for video.

Investing in a lighting setup beyond a simple LED light panel is usually based on a few factors like the light's throw (how well it can send light from one side of the room to the other), features they provide, or specialty-style lights used to light a speaker at events when directed from the rear of a conference room. For the average video content creator, LED panel lighting is more than powerful for any needs you'll likely encounter.

When to "Go Pro"

There's no greater feeling as you're uncovering the right gear for you than to see that gear in use and having your problems solved.

It's such a weight lifted from your chest when you can come into your recording space, sit down to record your content, and get back to the reason why you're creating videos in the first place, to share your business or your craft with the world.

If you're dedicating an entire space to recording content, and you're wanting a more singular light source that handles a lot of recording needs while providing soft, even lighting, I'd recommend you look into COB (Chip on Board) LED lighting setups with dome-shaped diffusion.

Of course, everyone always asks what I'm using for lighting my videos, and for the last three years, I haven't changed that setup from an LED lighting setup with spherical pop-up softbox lights that allow me to properly light any setup I create in my office and still have soft, even lighting like some other popularized lighting setups.

Plus, they don't take up a ton of space, and that's important to me.

CREATOR NEXT STEPS

- [ ] Evaluate your recording space and note existing lighting sources and where you can place your video lighting.
- [ ] Consider wall-mounted or table-mounting options when working in smaller recording locations.

RESOURCES

- Watch how white balance impacts the quality of your videos here: <u>**OneRightVideo.com/WhiteBalance**</u>
- Watch the video to see my current video lighting setup here: <u>**OneRightVideo.com/MyLights**</u>

Chapter 9

Choosing Your Ideal Camera Source

My first video was awful.

It was made on my cheap Android smartphone, aka a "dumbphone," and it was a disaster trying to record!

I was on a call with my business coach, and he told me that I needed to do videos and challenged me to record a video that day.

I can remember sitting on the phone thinking to myself,

"This guy does not know who he's talking to. I don't even take photos. How am I going to start making videos? Heck, I even recycle the same seven profile photos on Facebook every year like, 'I bet you guys didn't see this one!' as if no one remembers the picture."

Despite all the thoughts that crossed my mind, in what felt like an eternity but happened in milliseconds, I had one singular final thought before giving my reply - **I didn't hire him for me to remain the same.**

So, with nervous enthusiasm, I exclaimed to my coach, *"I'm going to do it."*

My coach was taken aback by my response and replied, "You're going to do it? You're going to make a video today?"

I eagerly and adamantly replied again, "I'm going to make a video today!"

When we got off the phone, my stomach dropped.

I went from my bare office to my living room, outside against the brick wall, corners of the walls–nothing looked right. Every angle I'd picked made me look like I was taking a booking photo at the police station.

I finally landed on recording the video in my car after looking through several YouTube videos to see common locations other people used. So, I figured, what the heck, it at least wouldn't look like I needed to have a serial number branded across my chest.

Into the car I went, on a 90+ degree St. Louis day with plenty of humidity and beads of sweat forming on my forehead and lips as I'd always remembered seeing Whitney Houston iconically wear during one of her many animated performances.

I turned on the air for a bit to calm my nerves and cool off the car for a bit, turned the car off after a few minutes to reduce any noise in the video, and hit the big red daunting button to record my very first video.

Whether you decide a smartphone or a dedicated camera is the right camera source for creating your videos, your camera is going to be one of the most important tools you'll leverage to create video content.

Buying the right camera can truly make or break your creation process.

It'll be the tool that either helps simplify video creation for you or frustrates you so much you quit prematurely.

It's now time to cover the third area of the A.L.V.A.S. Hierarchy of Investments to make sure you get the right camera the first time.

Finding Your Ideal Camera Source

Let me begin this chapter by sharing you will obsess about the camera above anything else.

There's probably the handful of readers that jump straight to this chapter, giddy to dive into cameras. I would be too.

There are so many camera options on the market, one would think if you pick up any one of them, you'd be good to go.

Needless to say, that's not so.

You're getting ready to begin a race and the camera you use is like starting over as a teenager with the putt-putt car that causes more problems than conceding to taking an Uber or public transit.

That's the perspective to keep in mind when using when choosing a prospective camera.

You can start with your smartphone; Ol' Reliable from your mom that works is great, but isn't the hot rod you dream about, but is plenty capable, and then some. However, it will require a little work to bring out the shine.

Then, there are some lower-end entry-level putt-putt cameras with the right accessories and constant workarounds can be pretty cool, some even fun to use. However, they don't come without some limitations. These are your cameras under $600.

The big brother higher-end entry- to mid-level cameras may still have their limitations, but offer more flexibility, have more features, and are relatively powerful. BUT (and a big but) just because you own the camera, doesn't mean you don't have to learn how it works to get the most out of it. These can range from $700 – $1,000 roughly.

Then, you begin to enter the Bee's Knee's Hall of Fame cameras with fewer and fewer limitations, and the difference between one camera body versus another are narrowed down to the camera's intended purpose. The mix of video and photo-based features will cause a difference in price.

The jump to $1,300 – $2,500 is where you find a sweet spot ideal for content-creating entrepreneurs because the limitations are minimal.

Deciding Your Creative Path

For the Non-Techy Entrepreneur Needing a Camera

Let's be 100% honest here.

If there's one thing true of most content-creating entrepreneurs, it's that you likely don't care that much about the gear.

You want the right tool that's going to do the right job and get on with your life, right?

I can empathize with that. For you, here's my short, sweet, and to-the-point camera recommendation – read the chapter so you're not completely in the dark about how to make an educated purchasing decision on choosing a camera.

Then, because you'll likely hire out the recording and/or editing job to someone else, invest in a camera that can survive your ideas and content goals. I'll share with you the baseline features your camera needs, and what to look for. Plus, my top recommendations will always be on my YouTube channel.

For Those of Us That Need to Know the Details & Are Gear Heads

You're in a safe space.

However, if your spouse or partner doesn't want you to buy any more gear, you've already messed up picking up this book friend. Just tell them any shopping you're doing at B&H Photo Video is really Better & Homes. That's the best I can offer ya.

My original attempt at writing this chapter would have caused your heart to leap with joy. Over 5,000 words of technical jargon, camera brand brow bashing, and the historical importance of each brand's reputation and contributions in the video content creation space.

Alas, dear reader, in the words of Sweet Brown, "Ain't nobody got time for that."

For that, I'd encourage you to join in the conversation on the Friday Live Help Casts on my YouTube channel, especially when new gear comes out.

And if you're knee-deep into the camera tech, but you're still not sure which camera to choose, take the camera quiz. It'll sort through my top recommended camera options for video based on your intended use case here: OneRightVideo.com/CameraQuiz

Are Smartphones *Really* Good Enough for Making Videos?

The short answer is yes.

If there's what feels like one timeless debate in the video space, it's the conversation of whether a smartphone is "good enough" to use as your primary camera source or do creators need to invest in a "real camera"?

When I first heard about this debate, I took the advice that my smartphone was good enough to record videos, and technically, it was... so why were my videos looking all fuzzy and terrible?

I quickly learned that just because it was a smartphone didn't mean I didn't need to learn to use it as if it were a regular video camera.

Some creators are still debating this question as smartphones worldwide constantly push the debate into the isle of irrelevance as new smartphone releases always include a significant amount of effort focused on the video and photo capabilities of the phone.

The bottom line is, **smartphones are awesome!**

Whether you decide it's right for you or not is a personal decision that boils down to a single word: **preference**.

Do you want to use a dedicated tool solely for videos or not?

For me, I found it difficult to document certain phone calls or wanting to vlog while in my car, and often needing my phone for something else phone-related.

Always needing to decide which held more priority in each moment of whether to use my phone as a phone or a camera was enough to make me buy a camera after a couple of videos with my then "dumbphone."

I didn't want to choose; I wanted both. So, I landed in the land of cameras and haven't looked back since. However, this is a decision you have to make.

I recommend getting a dedicated tool to do the job versus relying solely on your phone you'll need for other things than the camera.

The Great Camera Sensor Size Debate

The largest debate you're bound to encounter searching for the right camera for you is which sensor size is "the best."

Allow me to save you countless hours of "research," which is basically fellow creators explaining why they switched from one brand to another, what one camera has versus another, how much background blur one gets versus the other, and on and on.

It's a vicious cycle that can leave you more confused than when you started, plus you've wasted hours consuming videos based on the word of the day, **preference**.

An Easier Way to Digest the Difference in Sensor Sizes

The easiest ways I've found in explaining the three most common sensor sizes are like that of any American drive-through.

Think of sensor sizes like menu size options for french fries:

- Micro 4/3rds or M43 Cameras are your Small Sizes
- APS-C are your Mediums
- Full Frame are your Large Sizes
- and anything else, is usually a specialty of some sort.

Does this mean you're less satisfied the smaller the order, like with your food?

No, but each sensor size has some varying levels of limitations and differences, in addition to limitations camera models also have. To avoid a ton of confusion around what you can't see or make much of a comparison through reading a book, I'll keep these differences down to sensor sizes only and common differences they offer.

You'll often hear APS-C and M43 sensor sizes listed as crop sensor cameras because there's a difference between their size and the standard sensor size being full-frame.

You may be asking yourself if full-frame seems to be the standard, why not just use those and scratch the rest? Great question!

There are a lot of pros and cons to each sensor size, and each creator is different when it comes to their needs and why they prefer one over the other.

When you're considering what may be right for you in selecting a camera, the sensor size isn't the most important thing. The most important thing is that you select a camera that doesn't get in your way with limitations that are avoidable with a different or better camera option.

How Sensor Sizes Play Out in Real Life

For many creators, some enjoy full-frame cameras above all other options for videos, for a few common reasons:

— No crop on the video (we'll talk more about this later in this chapter)

— Increased shallow depth of field due to the larger sensor size (aka blurrier backgrounds)

— Great in lower-lit situations due to increased sensor size

With these options, it sounds like a great option, and it is. So what makes others want to take another route?

Budget, smaller camera sizes, smaller lens sizes, and, my favorite, less weight to lug around.

When you're going to decide on a camera, you'll want to consider how you plan to use your camera, and for a book nerd like me already carrying around a computer, a physical book, or allegedly multiple physical books, adding on an extra two to five pounds of camera gear isn't my cup of tea.

I think it's important to try each size in person if you can access them locally and decide for yourself. Or, uncover the inevitable truth, it's not as big of a deal as everyone makes.

Remember, these are photographers, indie filmmakers, and gear-focused tech enthusiasts majoring in the minor. We're not about that life.

The goal is not to get caught up in the 400% zoomed-in details to show a ladybug is slightly in or out of focus on a leaf. You're making videos for your business.

Remember to keep the main thing the main thing.

Sensor sizes should be a consideration when choosing your camera, but it's not at all ***the most important*** factor in determining the camera that's right for you.

Finding Your Near-Perfect Camera

Many camera-addicted creators constantly keep an eye out for "the perfect camera" but unfortunately, there isn't one undisputed perfect camera in existence.

All camera brands have their quirks, and while the perfect camera doesn't yet exist, it is possible to get as close to perfect for your specific needs.

Developing Your List of Non-Negotiables

This is the first thing I do when helping a client outline what the most important features are to pick the right camera for them and how they plan to create content for their brand.

a. How do you plan to create content?

b. What kind of content do you intend to create?

c. How long do you estimate your videos will be?

Think long-term about your content goals.

If you're only thinking one year in advance, you'll run the risk of investing money in a camera that's limited in its abilities to handle your current and future content goals. Don't let the idea of needing to pick "the perfect camera" send you into analysis paralysis.

We're going to break this down, so it doesn't stress you out.

When I ask most people what they plan to create, their first reply is "YouTube videos."

Think deeper.

The type of videos you intend to create could be videos of you showing new properties, traveling & sharing new experiences, creating craft or design videos, live-streaming, etc.

Consider what you intend to create 90% of the time. This will dictate what features you need for your camera to serve you the best. Think about the goals you have for your content and what you would like to do.

We'll choose your camera based on your goals.

Here are my Creator's Top 10 baseline features. I believe all creators need to have these features in their cameras, especially if your content focus is video.

1. A Flip-Out Screen
2. 4k Recording Capabilities
3. Reliable Autofocus in Video
4. Microphone Port
5. Headphone Port
6. Unlimited Recording
7. Clean HDMI Out (Native Live Streaming Capabilities)
8. Internal Power Charging
9. Image Stabilization (Digital or Internal In-Body Stabilization (IBIS))
10. Bluetooth and Wi-fi

There was a time when even half of these features were hard to find in a single camera body without spending upwards of $2,500 on the camera body alone, but now they are becoming more popular in some entry-level mirrorless cameras.

A common question I receive in my direct messages on social media is "What camera can I get for $300?" My answer is always the same:

"No camera that's not going to cause more issues than it'll solve."

Some cameras have a special set of features designed for specific creator goals like sports photography versus cinematography needs, and so forth.

One of my favorite cameras that broke the mold with this general pricing structure was the Sony ZV-E10. It included everything in my Creator's Top 10 feature set but for $700, which was unprecedented at the time.

But if you're asking yourself if you really need 4k video and some of these other features I listed, allow me to coach you through this process. Trust me, you're going to want these video features at your disposal.

Do you really need 4k in your camera?

There are always these silly debates online that pay too much attention to minor details versus the things that really matter. These are conversations that major in the minor.

When it comes to 4k videos, this is one of those subjects. The good thing is most modern mirrorless cameras have 4k video recording as a standard in cameras.

Do you need it? **Yes.**

Should your camera have it in the camera? **Yes.**

Does that mean you *absolutely* have to record everything in 4k? **No.**

Like any video other tool, 4k is a tool. And this, like many other tools, can be leveraged to help improve the quality of your video content quality.

Does this mean someone will skip your videos because it's in 1080p instead of 4k? Absolutely not.

But as the standard of quality changes online and as smartphones continuously edge out point-and-shoot cameras offering comparable features and often better quality, it's increasingly becoming more and more important to provide quality content not just information-wise, but visually.

When you're battling against various social media sites' compression, it's best to start with a high-quality video file like 4k, so when you distribute clips of your content to other sites like LinkedIn, TikTok, or Instagram, your videos don't go from great to mush.

YouTube also provides quality filter options when using their search feature, even providing a 4k badge on videos that are in 4k versus 1080p or Full HD videos.

As you're thinking of how you want your brand to be represented online and how much work you're putting into your craft, it's important to show up as your best, and not just as "good enough."

To put things into perspective, let me share with you a quick story of what happened when I was in college and only strived for "good enough."

Capture the 2%

When I went to college in Ohio, I had a full schedule that was jam-packed with classes, from the earliest classes were offered to classes later in the afternoon. My aunt consistently pushed my limits of what I considered "good enough" to pursue what was the best.

I had conquered my fears with mathematics, never getting less than a B+ on my assignments as I progressed on through college thanks to her coaching, and within a short time, became a star student from a mediocre student, at best, previously.

Entering a new semester, with renewed courage in myself, I felt confident enough to add on my next sets of classes that would eventually uncover my new nemesis, microeconomics, and a collegiate literary class that would eventually kick my butt.

Despite being fortified with my newfound courage and belief in myself, I began studying with other classmates after immediately recognizing I wasn't grasping the subjects as quickly as I would have liked, and set up a weekly study group.

From meeting at local shops to low-traffic areas of campus, and even each other's homes, as the end of the quarter was nearing, I finally felt confident in what I had learned in this weekly study group session.

As finals approached, the local news station predicted bad weather on what would be the day of my finals.

I was determined to make it to take this dag-on test after all the hard work I had put into studying, even breaking things off with a guy I was seeing at the time as things became too much to handle with everything I was working on.

The next day, I woke up to a blanket of pure powdery white snow completely covering every area outdoors. Armed with a steeping hot cup of freshly brewed coffee, I walked up to my car covered in easily 5-6 inches of snow, even on the nearby tree branches, and made my way to school to take my finals because, despite the weather, the exams weren't canceled. What might have equaled a city shutdown when I lived in Huntsville, Alabama was a normal day up north in Columbus.

I took the long, scenic route to school, leaving hours in advance to safely pull up to one of the few available spots left at the curb outside my class building. I parked the car and went out, ready to conquer the day, until I heard a faint hissing sound.

I raised my hat from over my ears, and it was now clear this hissing sound was coming from my car. It was perfectly silent outside, with no traffic noise at all, with only the sound of snow landing around me.

I walked around my car, inspecting it while asking myself, "Where is this noise coming from?"

I went back to my driver-side door to make sure it wasn't coming from inside the car and I looked down to see the front driver-side tire was pinched, and now slowly sinking, comfortably settling in the snow.

I couldn't believe it. Yet, I refused to let anything distract me mentally or emotionally from preparing to kick this test's butt. I turned around, determined to focus and study a bit before my class opened, still making it to school 40 minutes before the exam began instead of worrying about what was quickly becoming a flat tire on my car.

It was a couple of weeks later that I finally got my test result from the professor, and I was pumped! I scored a 98% on my exam!!

To me, this was proof positive that the work my aunt was doing with me to change my mindset was working, and I couldn't wait to get home and show her my test results.

I walked into the kitchen, glad to see she was already home, and I had to contain my voice to burst from yelling out and startling her with my great news.

"Auntie Shirley, guess what?!" I still partially yelled to her.

"What?" she replied, partially smiling, feeding off my grinning expression.

I popped out the test result to her and showed it to her like it was the Willie Wonka Golden Ticket. (Yes, I printed out the digital test results at school, so she could see and hold the results in her hands. What can I say? I was proud!)

"I did it!! I did just like you taught me, and all my studying and work paid off! I passed and with a 98%!" I said, of course by then yelling, brimming with excitement.

Without missing a beat, she replied, "What happened to the other 2%?" with a straight face.

I couldn't believe it. I was gutted.

Was she serious or just messing with me? "I don't know. What difference does it make? I have a 98%!" I reiterated, hoping she'd share with me how she really felt.

Little did I know she *was* serious.

My aunt replied in a straight, direct tone, "Do you know what you missed? Do you need to go back to tutoring to work on that some more or what happened with that bit?"

I was crushed. I felt defeated.

I could not believe she was really asking me what happened to this last 2% that I'd missed, as if it really mattered. Now I was starting to get a little pissed off. Was she seriously not going to congratulate me on all the hard work I'd done and advice I'd implemented from her on our compulsory regular weekend trips to run errands, regardless of my exhaustion. Not to mention books she forced me to read and report on, in addition to my regular school work.

"Auntie! What difference does it make? I worked my butt off for that 98%, and you're worried about some measly 2% that doesn't even matter?!"

My aunt always had an interesting way of communicating with me that lodged its way into my core memory system and would be something I would ponder and chew on for years to come. This was one of those moments.

She leaned in and looked me dead in the eyes.

"Diana. If you worked that hard and studied as much as I know you have been, you could have conquered that last 2% of the test. It's not that I'm not proud of the work you've done. I've seen you! You've worked hard, but if 100% is available, then why not go after the full 100%? Don't leave anything on the table. Capture the full 100%."

It was at that moment my aunt forever cracked my core belief system about "doing your best." Sometimes your best is not enough, and you must do what is required to succeed.

My aunt handed me back my paper, and I was still partially torn up about the information she'd just dropped on me in the middle of the kitchen. But in true auntie form, she handed me the paper back, attached with a warm hug, coupled with how proud she was of me.

I was truly numb at that moment and walked upstairs carrying my book bag and this 98% like an anvil attached to my arm. I felt defeated. But something was different. I closed the door to my room, refusing to turn the TV on or get on my phone. I just looked at this 98% like it was my greatest form of failure.

In an instant, I went from elated and proud to disgusted. I was determined to prove her wrong. Wrong about what exactly? I have no clue, but I know I wanted to show her I could get a full 100% because I deeply desired the approval of my aunt, who throughout all of my life has been one of my greatest champions.

My studying habits increased. My social time decreased even more than it was already for the introvert I was, and my personal TV time and *Call of Duty* video game playing time were now completely re-devoted to studying time. Every time I studied, I would find myself scoffing under my breath, "... tuh, 98%..."

Another quarter was coming to a close, and a new class was ending. I was determined. I wasn't going to just bring home a 100% test result; I had something else in mind planned.

I was going to show my aunt and win her approval that I literally already had from everyone else around me, but not from her, not really. I just couldn't shrug it off. From my parents, friends, siblings, even my uncle—they all congratulated my previous efforts of "the 98%" as it became named in my mind like a low-class peasant in a novel somewhere.

That Fall, my next quarterly results came back, and this time, armed with a second paper printed this time.

Walking in with a second shield to show my aunt who, again, had made it home before me, and it was like déjà vu. I walked in as brave as David facing Goliath and confidently held out the printer paper and handed it to my aunt while curiously looking at me.

No big fanfare, no smiles, just an outstretched arm followed by an intense glare, daring her to take it from my hand.

She laughed and smiled, looking at the paper. "I knew you could do it! See?!" she said proudly, embracing me with a tight hug; much more joy-filled than the one during the great 98% debacle.

Not only had I gotten 100% in several of my classes, but still struggling with the microeconomics class, I presented my aunt with official recognition that I had achieved the Fall Quarter's Dean's List.

I not only got the recognition for the hard work that I had done, but at that moment, it clicked what she had done and was trying to do inside of me all along.

It wasn't that she wasn't proud of the work I'd done previously, but she taught me how to stretch myself.

Not just for school, but in life.

The 98% wasn't about really missing the 2%, but going beyond your current "best" as a form of settling and truly stretching your belief about your capabilities from best to better than your best.

As she handed me back the paper, I was grinning from ear to ear, not only proud of what I'd accomplished but that I had also raised the ceiling of my belief system and stretched it beyond anything I could have imagined.

But not before she ended our conversation with, "Now, what about the President's List?" She smiled as she said it, though.

In video, it's not really a 4k vs 1080p conversation. 4k is here to stay with better resolutions constantly pushing the bar. And while there are technical reasons you can benefit from 4k, I pose the same question to you my aunt did me: When 100% is available, why settle for 98%?

Capture the 2%.

Which Camera Brands are Best?

If you haven't noticed by now, the camera and video space have endless ongoing debates, and another one to add to the list is which brand is best for video?

The most popular brands that produce mirrorless cameras used for video include Sony, Canon, Fuji, Nikon, and Panasonic.

All camera brands have their flaws and the niche market of creators they cater to the best. In this book, I'm only going to focus on those that best meet the demands of modern creators that are best for video. While there truly are no "bad" cameras, there are some that increase the ease of use versus others.

Warning

This is where a lot of creators that already have a camera or are starting to search for one will uncover that many creators have a personal preference toward one brand or another, and rightly so.

This brand loyalty will skew how each reviewer on YouTube reviews camera gear and equipment. Few camera reviewers are able to provide truly unbiased camera reviews without allowing their preference to alter their recommendation.

I am not exempt from this. However, my goal is to educate you on the features you need, the brands that do the best job at offering that, and provide options I think are best for content-creating entrepreneurs.

Some would profess, "All you need is..." or "XYZ camera model is overkill for most..." and for some select people, that may be right...*for them*.

However, when you have big content goals, you need tools that just work versus constantly searching YouTube for a workaround because of limited features from one brand of cameras or across certain models.

After trying and buying many cameras, I found a home with Sony's mirrorless line of cameras and haven't looked back since.

They're constantly leading the industry with new advancements in video performance, the world's fastest and most accurate auto-focusing systems on top of feature after feature that makes creating videos a breeze.

All camera brands these days offer great camera options. However, year over year, without question, Sony and Canon make some of the best cameras for content-creating entrepreneurs.

Compare Your Options vs Your List of Non-Negotiables

As new cameras are regularly released and new features become an almost must-have, when choosing a camera for video, compare what that camera offers versus your list of non-negotiable must-have features.

When you're considering what camera brand and model may work best for you in the style of content you intend to create, always consider FIRST your list of non-negotiables. Once you've done that, watch content from creators creating the style of content with the camera you're considering, and look at how easy or difficult is it for them to create.

Ask yourself:

— Are they constantly having to create workarounds for what are seemingly simple needs?

— Can you visualize yourself creating your intended form of content confidently without the camera interrupting your workflow with superficial limitations?

— If you accept the limitations of the camera you're considering, how will it impact how you create? Will that limitation make things easier, or more complex, or will you be unaffected?

The more cameras each brand released model after model, the more I saw the writing on the wall for me and which direction I needed to head to invest in a brand that had enough of a creative ceiling that it'd be some years before I even got close to maxing the capabilities of the camera I'd invest in.

Which Camera Is Right For You?

It's an ever-increasing trial to uncover which cameras have the best needs for my clients and audience, as new cameras are released every year, each with better features than the last.

To help you narrow down your options, because it'd be impossible to name a camera today that wouldn't quickly become displaced tomorrow, I created a Video Creator's Camera Quiz.

Every couple of months, it's updated and revised to include the best options available for video, already narrowed down to what I believe are the most creator-friendly models.

For an up-to-date listing of current and identifying your ideal camera, curated specifically for entrepreneurs, you can take the camera quiz here.

CREATOR NEXT STEPS

- [ ] Take the video camera quiz to identify which camera best fits your content creation needs.
- [ ] Revisit your list of non-negotiables from chapter 6 and note which camera best matches your list.

RESOURCES

- Identify what camera will be best for your content creation needs here: OneRightVideo.com/CameraQuiz

Chapter 10

Accessories: The Unsung Hero of Video

Accessories in the video space are like my favorite skillet I found years ago at that hotel liquidation sale.

They are not something you share on display and people never ask what pans you used when making a delicious meal, yet any good cook knows they're the staple to any functioning kitchen.

In the process of becoming a content-creating entrepreneur, accessories are the unsung hero of video creators all over the world, and why they're fourth in the A.L.V.A.S. Hierarchy of Investments after video cameras.

They're the silent worker in every setup that helps keep the wheels spinning and only receive attention when it's time to upgrade, or they break or fail.

What Accessories Should You Have in Your Setup?

What gear to buy, what videos to create, will your videos even be any good are all concerns and frustrations new creators run into. With so many questions at the front of your mind, accessories tend to always be on the back burner. However, they're some of the more important purchases you can make because it helps your system boil down into one word: reliable.

How well can you trust that the accessories you invested in can sufficiently support your camera and lens combo, whether for recorded or live-streamed content, are all determined by how well the accessories in that setup perform.

There are five primary categories when considering what you'll need in the accessories department:

1. Microphones
2. Lights
3. Cables
4. Storage & Data
5. Specialty tools

Already having covered the first two categories in previous chapters, we won't spend a lot of time on them here.

1. Microphones

Microphones are by far one of the greatest and most important accessories that you will have when creating videos.

Although microphones are included in the very first part of the A.L.V.A.S. Hierarchy of Investments, they actually are both an accessory as well as a primary element in video creation.

However, since we already covered microphones in-depth and audio within Chapter 7, feel free to go back through the audio chapter for more details on audio.

2. Lights

This is another one of the key performers of the A.L.V.A.S. system.

The reason lights also makes this list as well, as an important accessory to note, is to ensure you don't forget about lighting. Most new creators assume the ceiling light or side lamp in their living room or home office with a basic light bulb is good enough lighting when, in truth, it's not.

This is another one of the dedicated chapters we've already covered in depth in Chapter 8, so feel free to go back through that chapter to review tips on lighting.

3. Cables

On my Bee's Knees Hall of Fame list of accessories, cables by far outrank any other tool or accessory that you will invest in for video. The reason I rank such an elementary and basic tool so highly is because literally every piece of gear you will ever own needs a cable.

Whether that's a power cable, a cable for live-streaming, a cable for your headphones, connectivity, or extension cables—literally everything uses cables.

It's not until you're preparing to do an important live show or interview and you notice your laptop is progressively losing power despite being plugged in, or that your camera is about to die, or your audio isn't quite right—all because of the cable is broken or not connected properly. Ask me how I know.

The importance of excellent quality cables in abundance in your studio cannot be overstated. I don't feel bad at all in telling you to have three backup cables for each cable that you could possibly need. Because of how cost-effective and, frankly, cheap cables are, it doesn't make sense not to have three backups.

Here's a list of cables that you are going to need and use over the course of becoming a master video content creator:

1. USB-C to USB-C Cables
2. USB Micro Cables
3. Full-Size HDMI Cables
4. CAT 5 or CAT 6 Ethernet Cables
5. Camera AC Power Cables

These are just a few of the most commonly used cables that will attach to just about any type of equipment you're likely to invest in.

The best creator is a prepared creator.

No matter how big or small an opportunity is, I'm always prepared just in case something goes wrong with my setup, with backup equipment at the ready.

Oftentimes, many technical issues encountered during a recording or live session can be resolved by simply switching a cable. And without the right working cables, nothing works.

4. Storage and Data

If you can't save anything, you create anything.

Storage and Data definitely rank as another one of my top accessory must-haves for creators, because if you can't successfully save and retrieve the content that you're recording, you've basically just sat talking to yourself.

Trust me, I've done that enough times to know there's no joy in finding out your SD card is corrupt and the files from your camera are gone, or that you didn't properly save your footage after recording because something is wrong with your storage drive.

Ask me how I know.

There are a few forms of data that you will want to ensure that you have in your tool kit.

That includes:

1. Reliable SD Cards
2. Reliable SD Card Readers (to retrieve information from your SD card)
3. Reliable SSD Hard Drives
4. And Lord knows plenty of space in cloud storage solutions

This is not a request or an option; this is a must!

You **must** have reliable SD cards and data storage solutions if you're going to make it as a video creator and remain sane while producing video content.

SSD stands for **Solid State Drive**. Solid state drives do not include the traditional spinning disk inside like HDD drives. Solid state drives are much faster, more efficient, and less likely to become corrupt simply from dropping them.

An Expensive Lesson in Being Cheap

I had just purchased my very first camera that came with one of those "everything is included" kits on Amazon. It included a cheap SD card and no-name SD card reader, but I didn't know any better. I thought it was a good deal. That is, until I had to use them.

The SD card could not record content on my camera successfully without the camera producing an error saying that the videos I had just recorded were corrupt, meaning there wasn't a way for me to retrieve the videos I'd just recorded minutes earlier.

And when I *did* use the SD card reader, when I could successfully record content with the random brand SD card, it could not transfer the data I had recorded successfully to my computer without causing another error, with my audio and video being out of sync. When, in fact, I had recorded the video on the camera where it was perfectly in sync and had no issues.

This was when I learned the valuable lesson that when you buy too cheaply, you also buy the problems that come with being cheap.

5. Specialty Tools

If you grew up in the 90s or were a regular weekend or late-night TV viewer, you knew the value of a good infomercial. Phrases like "Set it and forget it!" became an iconic saying that everyone knows because underneath an often cheesy presentation was the solution to a common issue.

Fast-forward to today and the air fryer is the new must-have revolutionary tool. College students, busy moms, or health-conscious individuals all have an air fryer that solves a problem for them.

It's not that they don't already have a functioning oven, toaster, or even microwave; it's the unique spin on a simple solution of not having to heat the house by turning on the oven, and saving time or energy costs by having this small countertop appliance solves for millions of households.

In the video space, new inventions from many brands are what we'd consider the air fryer of the industry.

Items like the Rodecaster Pro 2 combine 4 to 5+ professional tools into one convenient package while simultaneously solving problems, much like the common air fryer does.

While there would simply be too many specialty tools (both hardware and software tools) to mention, here are some of my favorites in recent years that I use:

- Ecamm Live
- Loupedeck Live
- Rodecaster Pro 2
- Vocaster Two
- Ulanzi Quick Claw Release Plates
- The SwitchPod
- Rode Wireless Go 2

While this is always an ever-growing list, there are some tools and accessories you'll see created and advertised to video creators that simplify the many desires and frustrations creators have, and can make creating videos so much easier.

CREATOR NEXT STEPS

- [ ] Create a list of accessories that could save you and your team time or increase your workflow efficiency.
- [ ] What accessories can you invest in to become a more efficient video content creator?

Chapter 11

Software Saves Your Workflow

Efficiency Helps You Manage Your Time as a Creator

DISCLAIMER: Inefficient creators are the unhappiest creators that will begin a YouTube channel.

They'll end up feeling left behind every time they see a fellow creator celebrating their wins, they'll constantly be frustrated with every upload and eventually settle into the mindset of "*...If I just had the right tool...*" or "*...If I use what they're using (insert successful creator's name), then I'll start seeing some results!*"

This is the path that leads to wasting money, negative reviews, and complaints on all kinds of tools and courses. It is start of calling everything a scam.

The software tools you invest in are not a guarantee of success on YouTube and with your video content. In the same way, investing in tools like a hammer and saw to build a house doesn't automatically equal a house upon purchase.

You have to use the right tools, with the right skill sets applied, and time to build the house of content and success you desire. So don't get caught up in buying a bunch of software tools thinking they will make or break your success on YouTube, but the right tools *can* help you save time and become a more efficient creator so you can make educated decisions when creating versus throwing a bunch of stuff against the wall hoping something sticks and grants you success.

When you become aware of some of the most popular tools YouTube creators use to help research, create, and produce their content, you'll feel a glimmer of hope that maybe, just maybe, it'll work for you as well so you can accomplish your dreams and goals with your channel too. Well, I'm here to tell you that it can.

The right tools can help turn what used to take you three hours to complete into 15-minute processes, hours spent building reports or systems into easy one-click button functions. This is why software tools are the final step in the A.L.V.A.S. Hierarchy of Investments because they can help you build efficient systems when creating video content.

Let's dive into what programs you'll need and use most often as a creator from video editing, live-streaming, podcasting, and social media to save you time and money with wise software tools to make your workflow as a creator as efficient and income-producing as possible.

Video Editing Tools

Video editing software tools are by far one of the most important tools to go from an idea to a published video.

When you search the phrase "best video editing software for beginners" on YouTube, you'll find tons of results with lots of services from lots of creators. Once you contemplate what to use, you'll see what your favorite creators use, download a trial, and still be just as confused looking at the simplest software recommendation vs the more complex video editing software suggested on YouTube.

You may be asking yourself right now, "Which one should I choose?" especially since they all will look unfamiliar and a bit confusing.

When my first business coach recommended the video editing tool he used, I thought to myself, "Great! Now I don't have to worry about searching for what to use to edit!" I paid about 200 dollars for the software, downloaded it, and started looking for tutorials on YouTube on how to use it. To my surprise, there weren't many, and those I found weren't clear and easy to understand.

When you're considering a video editor, do a quick YouTube search and see what beginner-friendly tutorials there are on YouTube that look interesting and might be something you could see yourself following along with.

I always recommend to my clients to have something to actually edit a video with when you're considering a video editor. Simply *looking* at other people edit videos isn't all that helpful. Instead, having a video of yours that needs to be edited is an excellent way to do a trial run of the software and see how well it suits you.

Create Throw Away Videos

"Throw away videos" aren't videos that you'll actually post publicly to YouTube or social media, but are videos to practice creating and editing your content with so that you have actual footage you can make changes to when testing a video editing software. They're also to create practice recording videos for the first time.

If you want to learn a video editing software quickly, create a short two-minute or less video that you will actually post on YouTube.

This way, your intros, main video content, and every other element of a real video are present and will 10X your learning curve to go from thinking about how to create a video to actually seeing what it takes to create videos for your brand.

When considering what editing program might be right for you, ask yourself:

— Do I prefer something that I can easily drag and drop in images and graphics?

— Do I have goals of one day producing a short film or something major in the next two years or so?

— Will I edit primarily at home or in the office, or on the go and need a mobile workflow solution?

— Do I want something that's a one-time charge or something that frequently updates but has a monthly subscription charge?

Where and how you plan to create will dictate what direction you go in for choosing a video editing software. There really are no bad video editors, or at least none I'll mention in this book, that can't be used to create awesome videos that connect with your target audience.

Most software tools offer a free trial, allowing you to see how easy or complex the editor is. If you want to see my recommendations for the best beginner-friendly video editing software tools for creators, go here: **https://OneRightVideo.com/Editing**.

Choosing a Video Editing Software That's Right For You

Beginner & Intermediate Video Editors

Don't let the word "beginner" make you think these video editors aren't powerful. What makes the video editing software I'm going to recommend "beginner-friendly" is their user interface and being specifically built to make editing videos for the first-time user truly so easy that anyone can do it.

Some creators with 100k to 500k+ subscribers on YouTube still use these beginner-friendly video editors, so don't be afraid they'll hold you back from having a successful channel, because they won't.

iMovie Video Editor (Mac Only)

This is by far one of the most highly recommended beginner editing tools. It comes free with any Mac or iOS device because it's an Apple product they only allow on Apple devices.

As a long-time Windows and Android advocate, it gutted me to see a tutorial of how iMovie worked, only to learn at the end of the video it was Mac only. What was this, some special club where all the cool stuff was Mac only? I knew I had to find something that was Window-based.

iMovie is the baby sister to the big brother and professional video editing program, Final Cut Pro, but offers a similar user interface that is still easy to understand.

There's a reason it's the long-reigning champ in Apple's App Store as the #1 Free App. There are no in-app purchases and everything is free to use and operate with no pesky notifications to upgrade for more features.

Movavi Video Editor (Available for Windows and Mac)

Movavi is a great competitor to other similar companies, but a much better tool that's very similar in features and functionality.

All the same trimmings of stock footage, audio, and effects are also available in Movavi's own effects store.

This is by far the best editing software I think most creators should consider using when they're new because all the things I love about Final Cut Pro and the beginner must-haves of other tools are neatly packaged in Movavi.

When Should You Upgrade to a Professional Video Editing Software?

You'll know it's time to upgrade when your editing goes from being fun and fast to slow and increasingly frustrating.

When you get to a place where you're constantly wishing you could add in certain effects but can't, or you're dreaming up new ideas for your videos, but your video editing program of choice isn't capable of doing that idea, it's time to look at a more professional editing tool.

At times, it's better to wait until you hit this creative ceiling with your content and switch only after you're certain your chosen program isn't right for you or you recognize that hiring a video editor to edit your videos for you is actually the next right step instead.

But if you like jumping in the pool with both feet first, go straight for the video editing program you know you'll begin with and stay with long-term, versus bouncing around from tool to tool.

Professional Editing Software Options

Now here's where the fun begins, because whatever you can think of, the following editing software can execute them, albeit with the right skills and effects.

There are three primary editing suites to consider when you're ready to use professional editing software:

➢ Adobe Premiere Pro

➢ Final Cut Pro

➢ Davinci Resolve

These three juggernauts are masters with color grading, keyframing, adding effects, audio controls, adding animations, green screen effects, and more!

You can't go wrong with any one of these options, but there are a few pros and cons to each that may help sway you to one camp or another.

Both Premiere Pro and Davinci Resolve work on both Mac and Windows machines, with only Final Cut Pro restricted to macOS only.

All three programs are true professional editing tools used on major motion films like *Deadpool, Spider-Man: Far From Home, X-Men Origins: Wolverine, The Girl with the Dragon Tattoo*, and more.

Indie filmmakers, content creators, and brands everywhere use these three programs the most to create content daily and award-winning short films, like one of my favorite short films called *Sriracha* by Griffin Hammond.

While the various pricing models of these software tools can help persuade your decision, it shouldn't be the only factor in deciding what you choose.

Desktop computer options are only one set of options available to creators. The advancements of the modern smartphone also come with it, powerful new processors and capabilities more advanced than what Alfred Hitchcock used to create his masterpieces, all available in the palm of your hand.

Mobile Editing Options

It used to be that editing on a smartphone was looked down upon as if they were just "for fun" and not for serious work. Today, that's a very different story with the power of modern smartphones.

They're incredibly powerful and have become the ultimate "gatekeeper remover" when coupled with the internet. It's poorly looked upon these days if a company *doesn't* have a mobile-optimized version of their software or tool unless it's specifically made for desktop only.

Mobile apps like LumaFusion and Filmic Pro have changed the game of what's possible when creating with a smartphone.

Some of the best tools available when you're traveling and on the go with mobile content creation include:

— **Filmic Pro** | Gives you mirrorless camera features on your smartphone.

— **LumaFusion** | The absolute best mobile video editor I've seen. Basically Final Cut Pro X on mobile.

— **Videoleap** | A full-scale video editor for Android and iOS.

— **Adobe Lightroom** | Adobe's mobile version of its photo editor that's very powerful.

There are tons of mobile apps available in the Apple and Google App Stores, but not all are great.

A few things to watch for with less commonly known apps are things such as:

— **Checking the Apps Reviews** | Reviews are a great way to see if an app is littered with spam, malware, or never-ending ads.

— **Check the Apps Update History** | I love to find a new app and see the developer released recent and regular software updates and bug fixes.

This lets me know the creators care about what they've put out into the world and are listening to their users by adding new or highly requested features.

CONS

Right now, you may be saying to yourself, "Diana, this is all so great, but if phones are so versatile and great, why don't you use one to create content?"

Well, my friend, I'm glad you asked. I actually started my content creation journey on my smartphone. Although it lacked so many features, it honestly could be called a "dumbphone" instead of a smartphone.

I tried it, and I *hated* it!

The video quality was awful, and the mic cable needed to be excessively long to reach from where I sat to reach the phone. Wireless microphone options that didn't cost a fortune just weren't a thing back then. So, while smartphones were versatile, they were also a pain for the would-be efficient creator.

It'd take me far more than twice the time to create on my phone or even edit than it did on my computer and using a camera.

This is where you learn which team you prefer to be on, team desktop or team smartphone.

The "cons" when using a smartphone as your camera and video editing source really depend on what kind of creator you want to become.

This is a biased reason, but why I hated using my phone as a camera:

- It was increasingly inefficient to transition from working or normally using my phone to being able to just sit down and create a simple video.
- Transferring the video file from the phone to my computer is a much slower process versus using removable storage options.
- The battle to keep my phone charged while creating, even with the use of smartphone accessories to mitigate that, was increasingly annoying.

The "cons" I listed are based on my preference and experiences only. For some creators, mobile is faster and more convenient for them.

Only you can decide what kind of creator you are and if it's right for you. I always suggest to my clients and new creators to try creating 10 videos with their smartphone. If you find you hate it and just wish you had a dedicated camera, get the dedicated camera instead.

CREATOR NEXT STEPS

- [ ] Outline a simple creative content plan to fully test the efficiency of a software tool during the trial period.

RESOURCES

- Identify which video editing software will best fit your creative needs here: OneRightVideo.com/Editing.

Phase 4 | Video Content Creation Strategies

Chapter 12

Winning the Battle of Being Consistent

There are a myriad of reasons why entrepreneurs find themselves stuck in a creative rut and in one of the following camps:

1. "I have all these ideas, but I don't know what to do with them or how to create videos."
2. "I've bought a ton of gear and trying to figure out how to use it frustrating me."
3. "I have all the gear, I keep buying more, but when I think to go create a video, I freeze up."
4. "I really don't have the time to create videos. It'd take too much time to do."

If you find yourself in the fourth camp, re-visit chapters 4 and 5 where this concern is specifically addressed.

The interesting truth is all of these concerns are based in one fundamental root issue, fear.

To audibly admit and say the words "I'm afraid" isn't something the average person wants to say or feels comfortable saying. It's far more comforting and acceptable to say other phrases that push the word "fear" to the back of line.

If "not having the right gear" is the problem, then fear never has to be addressed because it allows you to go through endless amounts of videos on YouTube and invest in gear until you find "the perfect" gear; whether it be cameras, lights, or accessories.

If learning to use the gear is the problem, the result can still be the same, watching endless videos and searching for "the right tutorial" that will finally show you how to use your equipment. Then, blame can be shouldered with the tutorials on why a video hasn't been created yet.

Finally, if finding "the right strategy" is the reason why it means avoiding the concern of wasting money, which surely none of us could ever be accused of, right?

The truth is fear is the common culprit here and without addressing the real cause, you'll find yourself wading through symptom after symptom, never addressing the real cause.

Because you already have a business or brand you're building outside of YouTube, you likely already have a core reason why it's important to you to help reach a wider audience and connect deeper with the people that need you the most.

I would encourage you that all you need to do is two things:

1. Recommit to **why** this is important to you.
2. Commit to creating video content versus it being optional.

When you commit to creating content, you remove excuses from the equation.

All excuses are equal.

You've done far greater and more complex things in life you've simply marked off in your mind as "common" and have overlooked how incredible you are.

Consider things you likely have done in your life:

- Learned how to go from being a young adult to a mature adult living on your own.
- Learning to drive a dangerous motor vehicle that kills thousands every year, but you fearlessly drive regularly.
- Applied and went to college; whether in-state or out-of-state as a teenager or young adult.
- Got married, not knowing the first thing about how to have a long-lasting successful marriage.
- Had children and begun to raise them, likely never taking a parenting course or doing extensive research on how to do this.
- Applied for jobs and pursued a career.
- Started a business and likely have other individuals whose livelihood relies on the success of this business.

Somewhere in the history of your life, no matter how old you are, you've likely experienced worse trials in life than creating a YouTube video that you achieved simply because you made the decision to.

I could share with you strategy after strategy, but none of them would work if you aren't committed to doing this for your own reasons.

For some, that means being honest with yourself and reaching deep down for why creating these videos on YouTube is important to you and committing to not letting distractions get in your way.

No video ever jumped up and socked someone in the eye, so you're in no mortal danger, but your dreams and aspirations are.

To create The One Right Video, you need to first commit to being consistent and not letting distractions get in your way, and right now, fear is a distraction.

You've learned to do a lot in life already, you can learn video.

All distractions are equal. ~ Diana G.

Remember from the earlier chapters in this book about the goldfish and the shark?

Let's get you some shark teeth to equip you to create.

CREATOR NEXT STEPS

- [ ] Create a list of common distractions you encounter weekly that distract your from your goals. (You cannot list your kids. 😁)

- [ ] Write out a simple way your **best self** plans to stay focused this week, and achieve your content goals.

____

____

____

Chapter 13

Never Lose Another Video Idea

Ideas are like unrefined diamonds.

There are 5 key sections to start taking ideas you have about the type of content you could create from your mind into a bingeable video on YouTube. As you've progressed through various chapters in this book, you've progressively acquired elements that will help you create *The One Right Video*.

As we progress through the next several sections, start capturing your ideas as you have them; don't wait. There's nothing worse than a forgotten great idea.

Secondly, actually do the exercises recommended. My phrase **Learn & Do** isn't just a cute saying but the absolute best way to learn and retain what you're learning, no matter your personality type.

Why? Because however you personally learn best still requires you to *do* what you've learned.

I would imagine you didn't pick up this book just for a little light reading, but to achieve a specific end result goal. I intend for you to achieve that goal progressively as you read and complete each chapter and the exercise within.

It's now time to start transforming your ideas into structured and bingeable YouTube videos.

Here's an overview of what we'll be covering:

1. Idea Capturing
2. Organizing & Researching Your Ideas
3. Planning Your Videos
4. Structuring Your Videos
5. Releasing Your Videos on YouTube

Ideation & Organizing Your Ideas

In Chapters 4 and 5, we covered an easy way to capture your ideas and organize them by the estimated time commitment using the Content Quadrant so that you can create them no matter how busy you get.

To recap, here's the idea capturing folder structure covered:

1. Capture
2. In Progress
3. Done/Recorded

As you capture your ideas, to know how long it'll take to create the various content pieces, separate them into the four areas of the Content Quadrant, which are:

➢ **Quadrant 1:** Quick Hitters

➢ **Quadrant 2:** Light Planners

➢ **Quadrant 3:** Medium Planners

➢ **Quadrant 4:** Hard Hitters

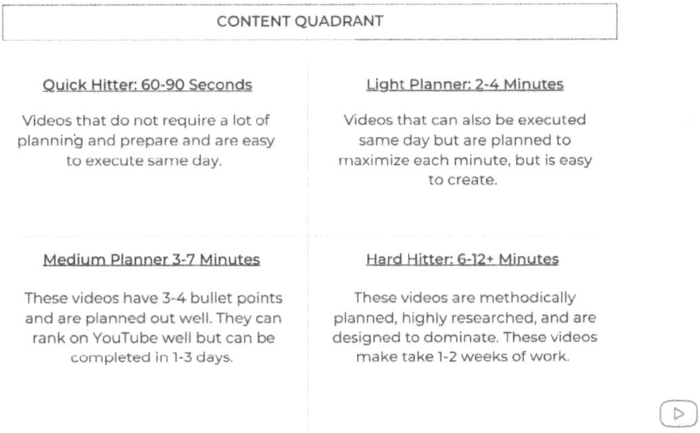

Identifying Your Channel Promise & Primary Content Pillars

As you begin to capture more of your ideas, it's important to have your content pillars identified.

This can seem backward, assuming your content pillars should be first, then capture your ideas and assign what content quadrant that idea is best suited to. However, if you don't have your content pillars identified, you can't properly build your content funnel.

If you spend too much time trying to initially organize an idea, you run the risk of losing the potency of the idea or losing the entire idea. It's best as you're having ideas to simply load them into the Capture folder and organize them later.

Step 1: Identify Your Core Channel Promise

To build a creative structure you can easily funnel your ideas through, your content pillars must first be identified. **Content pillars** are the primary categories your content ideas are best organized into. To minimize the risk of your content being too broad on your YouTube channel, you need to understand why your ideal viewer wants to watch your content and why they'd return to your channel.

This is best siloed into your channel promise statement by answering: who are you helping with what specifically?

This statement originally learned from my business coach is pregnant with making it easy for viewers to know what you do and why should they care.

Who = Your Ideal Target Audience/Client

Helping to Achieve = What is the Transformation the Viewer Will Receive?

With What Specifically = How Will It Help Them Specifically?

You want to become your ideal target viewer and client's go-to resource. To do this, your channel cannot be confusing where they have to guess the type of content you'll create.

If you're a social media expert, it could be helping local businesses bring in an extra $15,000 per month based on their social media content strategy.

For a direct sales copywriter, it could be helping online course creators double their enrollment by correcting their sales pages.

Answer the following to begin developing your content pillars:

Who are you helping?: ____

With what specifically?: ____

If your answer to who you're helping is "everyone" or "people who want to...", be more specific.

For example, on my YouTube channel, my core target audience is busy entrepreneurs learning video content creation. Because my channel covers cameras and video editing programs, it easily draws in photographers, indie filmmakers, and similar creators. However, they are not my target audience.

Your content should always be attracting and repelling at the same time. You want to attract the right ideal viewers and repel those that are not your target audience.

Of course, they're welcome to watch, enjoy, and engage with the content, but when you're structuring your videos, you want your ideal viewer to ***know*** this video was made for them.

Being specific drastically enriches the quality of your content and makes the conversion process of turning viewers into clients much easier.

Step 2: Write Down All Your Ideas & Questions Your Ideal Viewer is Struggling With

Based on your channel promise statement, how will you achieve this aim?

The easiest way to identify this is to start by writing down what are the common problems and questions your audience deals with.

- What are the pressing questions they have or are struggling with?
- What are the type of questions your best clients have asked?
- What are recurring questions you're asked over and over?
- What tools or programs would they use that are confusing them?

The key is getting down to core problems and challenges they're having and the real issues they're dealing with that are topical questions but also deep core issues they have that are keeping them up at night.

As an entrepreneur, your business already serves a purpose in helping an ideal target audience. This likely isn't going to change much as you're identifying your channel promise. You want to build a channel that, when your ideal viewer is exposed to your content, they instantly know they need to subscribe based on the channel content, even if your channel is new.

Set a timer for 15 minutes and write down all the ideas and questions that come to mind.

Write without stopping and don't pre-judge your ideas as good or bad; just write.

The most helpful ways I've found to do this is to grab a stack of sticky notes and write an idea on each notepad or grab a sheet of printer paper and draw a mind map. Don't try to organize these ideas right now; just note them down.

Seriously, don't go researching any special software tools to use or search out some YouTube tutorials on the best way to do this. That's nothing more than a distraction right now.

If you use a digital assistant like Alexa or the Google Assistant, ask it to play some soft music for 15 minutes, and when the time is up, the music will simply stop versus using an alarm, which is more jarring, and frankly, annoying.

Choose wordless audio so you're not distracted by the song you're listening to. If you're typing on your phone or computer, put it in a "do not disturb" mode so you're not distracted by any alerts or notifications.

Step 3: Categorize Your Ideas Into Content Pillars

If you look through the notes you have, you'll see some common themes that stand out.

Organize these into the top three to five main themes that stand out. To download the worksheet to help organize your ideas into content pillars, go here: OneRightVideo.com/ContentPillars

Have you spotted the flaw with this exercise yet?

If you followed through with completing this exercise, you will have noticed some content ideas aren't strong enough to either fit into their own content pillar without creating a rabbit hole of ideas that derail you from your main channel promise or you've created too many content pillars.

Sticking with three to five primary content pillars is best or you run the risk of watering down your content, causing your viewers to struggle with identifying how exactly your channel will help them.

These "stragglers" aren't bad ideas; they are instead what are considered associated and related content categories.

Let's say you're a real estate agent helping first-time home buyers get their first home in half the time of other agents. Your top three to five content pillars could be financing tips or advice, the home searching process, FHA applications, loan programs, etc.

Navigating various websites necessary to the viewer's success or things to watch out for when going through the application process are essential to the type of content you'll create. A natural associated or related content pillar would be how to navigate various websites.

While you don't need to be an expert in every small detail of how to use all the websites and programs in the process of applying, identifying core questions your audience would ask when using this site become great video ideas you can create.

Step 4: Use Your Audiences Language

It's right at this moment when I'm working with clients where they get a surge of creative juice flowing and want to jump right into creating content. Hold on to that energy. We're going to transform that energy from a shotgun approach to a laser that will hit its target.

Content Distribution Types

When you're forming your ideas into video ideas or possible titles of the video, you must think from the perspective of the person on the keyboard, not as the expert.

When you're thinking as "the expert" only, you're not thinking that the words or phrases you use as jargon, but it's likely in a format your viewer won't initially understand.

We'll dive deeper into planning your videos shortly but the next step in planning your video content is determining your core content distribution types. Your **Core Content Types** are the primary ways you'll create your content. This could be via your regular YouTube videos, your video podcast, or your live streams.

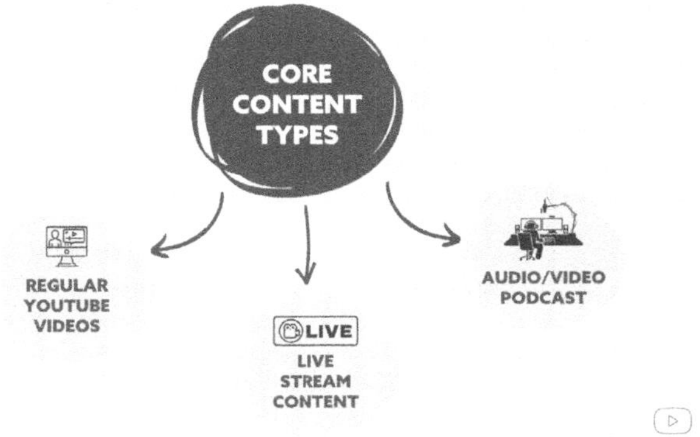

The ideas you've generated at this point could easily fit into any three of these core content types, however, here's a simple way to know how to segment those ideas.

Regular YouTube Videos can be any of the ideas you've written. You can also take well-performing videos and extend the conversation into a live stream or video podcast.

Live streams are great for ideas that can be restructured into open-ended conversations with your audience or covering in-depth concepts while addressing questions from your audience live.

If there are exciting updates in your niche or breaking news-type updates, you can truly connect with your audience in a way recorded content alone simply cannot accomplish.

Audio/Video Podcasts are great for expanding and going more in-depth to have a conversation with your audience. Even if you've covered a specific topic in a regular YouTube video, you can always expand on that topic in a podcast format.

Outlining Your Ideal Customer Journey

There are other content delivery formats like deciding if you want to also cover that format in a micro-content social media piece or if you want to cover that concept in a vlog-style format.

You can have a video idea that works for any format, but what dictates how you share your video idea is partly determined by learning how your audience prefers to be communicated with.

If every video is a long 30-minute YouTube video for what could be a 5-minute video, your audience will become frustrated. And inversely, if you create a short video on something they expect you to slow down and share the step-by-step in-depth details for, they'll equally become frustrated.

The way you learn the best way to deliver content to your audience is by understanding their customer journey path.

If you're our real estate agent from before and your target audience is first-time buyers in the homeownership market, using words they likely haven't learned yet based on where they are in their customer journey is a disservice to them.

When you assume, you tend to make an ass of yourself.

A **customer journey** is simply the path your ideal target audience or viewer is traveling in which the beginning of that path is where they are starting from and the end of the path is where you're leading them to.

The end of the journey could be where you no longer assist clients.

For example, the first-time homeowner now wanting to own commercial real estate properties may reach the end of their journey with you helping them because first-time homeownership may be the extent of how you help them based on your expertise and preference. Then, that customer begins a new journey elsewhere.

Or, it could be the coaching client of a social media marketer who continues working with you long-term because the journey to leveraging social media content means continuing to adapt to changes in social platforms, features, and analytics.

It's not uncommon to recognize the scope of your channel promise and your business serves two different ideal target viewers of which one is a beginner and the other is more experienced.

As an entrepreneur, you likely are already familiar with how your business best serves your ideal client. However, now you're entering the content creation space, and making assumptions is a double-edged sword. We don't want to assume; we want to *know* our content will resonate with our audience.

To identify your customer's journey and ensure you're operating with extreme clarity, look at the list of ideas you've been capturing and writing down. Are these the questions from someone that's brand new learning about your content topic or someone at an intermediate or advanced experience level?

CREATOR NEXT STEPS

- [ ] Outline your primary 3-5 Content Pillars in your business using the Content Pillars worksheet.

RESOURCES

- Download the Content Pillars worksheet here: OneRightVideo.com/Editing.

Phase 5 | Video Marketing Strategies

Chapter 14

Planning Your YouTube Video

One of the best things I could have done for my creativity was to post a large piece of craft paper on the wall to write down ideas as I had them.

Writing on paper with no lines is highly underrated.

When you write in a space that is unstructured, it allows you to connect the dots so much better than writing on paper with lines. If you're one of my iPad or tablet creators that love to use this digital resource, break away from this for the short time you're working through this book.

Why? Because **all distractions are equal**.

Having your ideas intercepted because of notifications, a steadily decreasing battery life, and the ability to easily switch from your notes app to something else when you have a squirrel moment and your mind wanders isn't going to be as helpful in this next stage. Just trust me on this.

Researching Your Content Ideas

Look at your content ideas sheet and see what ideas in your content pillars go together.

For now, let's take three video ideas that are similar and build on them.

Before you ever begin to create a video or plan out what goes into the video, capture the ideas you have in the notes **Capture** folder, but don't record it until you've first gone through the research steps for your video.

I like to break my research down into simple duplicatable steps:

1. Validate the Idea
2. Speak the Audience's Language
3. Identify Their Right Now Pain Point
4. Note What Areas Were Uncovered While Researching That Should Be in a Follow-Up Video
5. Filter My Video Idea Using the C.L.A.R.I.T.Y. Content Framework

Validating the Idea

In the validation phase, the main thing I want to ensure is that my ideal target viewer that I want to become my client is actually challenged with the idea concept I'm presenting as a possible content topic.

My main concern is making sure I'm listening to the occasional silent majority versus the loud minority.

Imagine getting ten comments, all saying I wish you'd make a video on X. You'd think ten is a lot of people, and in some respects, it is.

However, you could have a content idea that would better serve the 1,000 who are experiencing a challenge but just haven't verbalized it on your channel yet. This is what I call the silent majority.

It's about paying attention to the unspoken desires of the sometimes silent majority because you've identified their pain points, what they're struggling with, and what's confusing them versus the one or two comments or emails you received on another issue.

I love to begin all my validation searches on YouTube, in the YouTube search bar. YouTube's prediction engine will start triggering the most commonly searched phrases, questions, and keywords based on other users searching on the platform.

If you type in "LinkedIn," you'll see the search prediction engine also suggests: LinkedIn tutorial for beginners, LinkedIn Profile, LinkedIn marketing, etc.

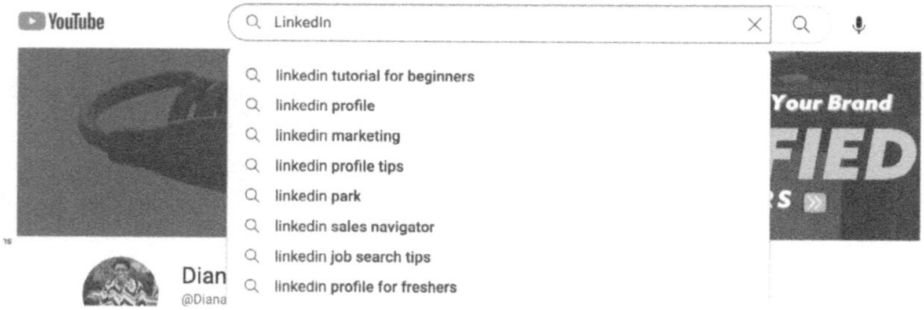

When you get more specific, you'll see results surrounding the specific phrase or word.

If you went back to the YouTube search bar and typed in "LinkedIn marketing," you'd now see: LinkedIn marketing for business, LinkedIn marketing 2022, etc.

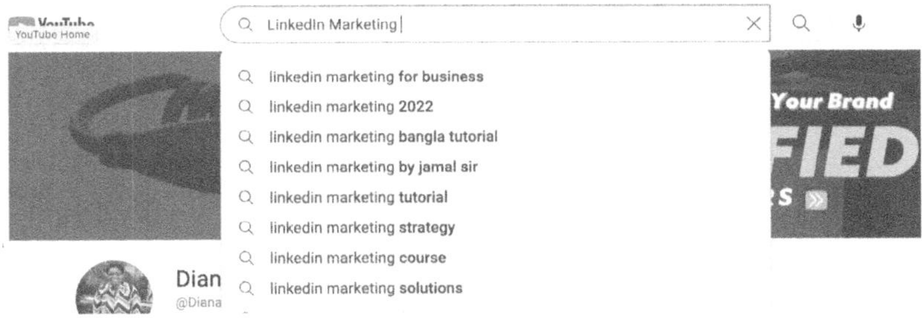

What I'm looking for when initially typing in the specific keyword or keyword phrase is how the phrasing is worded, what order it's typed in for relevance, and other similar or surrounding ideas that I can generate from the other prediction results.

It's easy to assume those typing in "LinkedIn marketing for business" are also typing in and looking at results for "LinkedIn marketing tutorial" and "LinkedIn marketing strategy" coupled with the year for relevancy of up-to-date strategies versus those from 2018, for example.

What you want to look for is the story or logic chain that the ideal viewer is in when typing in your specific keywords or phrases.

- What mindset are they in that they'd ask this type of question?
- Where does this place them in their customer journey?
- Based on your channel promise and business services offered, how can you serve them when addressing this topic?

When researching specific phrases, be careful of getting too narrow in your phrase. Those often seeking to rank first in the YouTube search results either are too broad or far too narrow.

Ranking first on YouTube for a phrase that isn't highly searched or isn't interesting at all to your ideal target audience at all is counterproductive to your content goals on YouTube.

When looking at YouTube search results, I'm also looking at other factors in the **content validation step** like:

- How many recent videos have been made on this topic?
- How up-to-date are the tips/information shared in these videos?
- How much traction are the top 10 videos getting covering this topic?
- If I were my ideal target audience struggling with this issue, which of the videos do I see appear the most interesting? Why?

When reviewing the content, the next step is to watch the top-performing videos and those that appear the most alluring with two perspectives:

1. As the person on the keyboard searching for answers (your ideal target audience)
2. As the researcher (the content-creating entrepreneur)

When reviewing fellow creators' videos, ask yourself:

- What information does the creator assume the viewer knows?
- What information is being omitted in this video or poorly explained?
- Is the viewer left with a sense of relief or forced to continue watching more videos to address other questions they have?

Speak Your Audience's Language

Once you've reviewed the video, take some time to scroll through the comments section of each video and note what questions are being asked, what concerns are being raised, and what frustrations are noted in the comments.

Comments aren't always gospel because similar to what can happen on your video is having the wrong target audience be attracted to the video where they assume it was made for them, and it wasn't. This can happen on any channel, so be mindful of that.

Evaluate the content you see in the comments section and why the viewer would ask certain questions.

Identify Their Pain Point

If a video covering the latest strategy for Instagram marketing had 100 upvotes next to a comment that said, "I expected to see more on Instagram live strategies, but you completely skipped over it and have no videos on your channel about it either."

This is the type of comment I'm going to make note of when researching content because I want to see what statements, comments, or complaints others resonate with.

Also, make a note of exactly how viewers are commenting when validating video content.

Don't limit your search only to YouTube; also look across other social platforms when researching content topics. Some untapped resources to get information from the horse's mouth are Twitter, Reddit, and TikTok.

What makes these three specific platforms amazing for content research is that viewers comment with zero filters.

I want to know how frustrated they are, how they're phrasing their questions, and what language they're using to describe their pain points surrounding that topic–even if it's the incorrect jargon for your niche. When you write sales copy to promote your services online or in your videos, use their words, not jargon.

In researching your content ideas, pay attention to what needs to be included in that specific video being planned and what needs to be added to a separate video to avoid overstuffing the content.

As you begin to put the details together to develop what concepts should be included in your video, it's now time to structure your video into the five stages that will make for an engaging video.

CREATOR NEXT STEPS

- [ ] Search common phrases relevant to your niche in the YouTube search bar and evaluate replies in the comments section.
- [ ] Evaluate the types of questions, concerns, and responses beneath videos in your niche, and perform the content validation tips.
- [ ] What are common pain points your ideal target viewers are mentioning?

Chapter 15

How to Create Videos People Love

How do you start a video?

After I bought all the camera gear and got a halfway decent image (if I'm being polite to describe how awfully ugly the first videos with my camera were) was the main question broadcasting across my forehead.

"How do I even make this video?" I kept asking myself, looking at the red recording light as time ticked away filling the memory card with blank stares at a camera.

3 minutes – 5 minutes – 7 minutes.

I kept watching the time add up with only utterances that made me sound drunk or completely aloof about "the right way" to introduce myself or begin this stinking video. I dare say Ariel from *The Little Mermaid* did a better job her first day on dry land, and she couldn't even speak.

Allow me to save you the dramatic hell and weirdness to not only begin your videos in an engaging way but to also structure them so your audience loves and enjoys them without feeling like you need a therapy session from trying to create content.

Getting Started Creating Videos

.....can you keep a secret?

That – that right there is how you begin a video. Let's try another one.

- **For Anne, he'd risk everything.**

Let's do one more.

- **He'd kill her for knowing the truth.**

Okay, I took a little literary liberty with that last one, but these are what you'd call a hook.

A **hook** is the opening line or phrase used to capture the attention of the audience and drive them from one line to the next, from one second to the next. The **intro** is the first initial segment of a video that houses the hook.

This is also just plain ol' good copywriting and that's what a good video is, a visual representation of copywriting in action.

It's the ability to play the game of capturing and keeping your audience's attention as you progress from section to section in a video.

The first few sections of a video are the most crucial.

Unless that viewer already knows, likes, and most importantly, trusts you to deliver on why they clicked, you're on the clock, whether they're desperately searching for answers on YouTube or mindlessly scrolling until they see what's interesting enough to click.

The thumbnail catches the eye, the title coupled with the thumbnail convinces them to click, and the length of the video has to be worth it.

This is the social behavior of the viewer on YouTube.

A consumer's normal behavior on a social platform is what I define as their **social behavior**. From how they analyze what to pay attention to, how they typically behave when interacting with that content, and what the viewer's expectation is while on that platform.

On YouTube, a viewer will typically discover your content a few different ways:

- By suggestion, based on your YouTube watch and search history
- From the YouTube search results
- From the YouTube suggestions based on related content
- Discovery via YouTube Shorts content
- and various methods of shared content on and off the platform.

With tons of options to shop around and watch on YouTube, and multiple options still enticing them to click away, you can see how increasingly important it is to keep the viewer's attention.

What is The One Right Video?

I'm sure when you initially saw this title, you wondered, What is *The One Right Video* and how do I create it?

To this point, unless you have a strong core mindset, the obstacles of your time and gear cleared, creating *The One Right Video* won't work.

Sure, you can still execute the three elements I'm about to share with you and have varying levels of success, but not consistent success.

Why?

Because people quit on themselves more often than they ever have any job they despised. Video is already the shortcut to the shortcut, but YouTube is playing the long game.

These strategies will work on any video type, including social media micro-content on other platforms. If you've made it this far in this book, you're in the minority of most people who buy books and actually finish them.

So, congratulations!

I would say it's like winning the Willie Wonka Golden Ticket, but it wasn't white chocolate in that candy bar, so that's not good enough. Instead, consider this the Bee's Knee's Hall of Fame, the greatest achievement known to man, or at least on my YouTube channel.

The One Right Video is composed of three elements:

1. 4 Steps to a Killer Intro
2. 5 Pillars for Creating Content People Love
3. Filtering the video with C.L.A.R.I.T.Y. Content Framework

You've likely had some part of this framework in your video and the first two are relatively common, but here's where creators mess up:

- The intros are far too long and bloated with uninteresting content.
- The main parts of the video the viewer desires to see are hidden in a mess of irrelevant information they don't care about.
- The video is too long or too short, omitting the bits they actually desired to see when they clicked the video.
- Relevant elements of the video's promise is purposely omitted to force

the viewer to watch another video versus giving them what was originally promised in the current video.

The most helpful bit of information to remember on YouTube is that the viewer doesn't care how much you spent on gear, how much of an expert you say you are, and doesn't care about irrelevant credentials.

From the moment they click on your video, they only care about one thing: Do you have their answer?

If you answered yes in your mind, your video has to prove that answer. If the viewer doesn't believe you, then to them, you don't have their answer. This can be harsh to hear, but it's the truth.

All videos have a job to do, and without holding that person's attention long enough to show you have their answer, the video cannot achieve its goal. The goal is to show them this video isn't going to waste their time and attention.

And to honor your time and attention, let's get to work!

4 Steps to a Killer Intro

The power of a strong hook or intro (these will be used interchangeably to mean the beginning of your video) is to capture and keep their attention to transition them into the next section of your video.

Because viewers have been consistently disappointed with intros being a complete waste of time, they've developed the social behavior to skip and scan through the video until they find the main reason they clicked on the video.

If you've watched any tutorial content on YouTube analytics, you'll hear that officially YouTube considers the first 30 seconds of the video as the intro section of the video. However, more and more viewers are finding less and less value to watch the first minute or so of a video.

When viewers begin skipping various parts of your video, this hurts what's known as audience retention on YouTube. **Audience retention** is how long you maintain the viewer's attention when watching your video.

When you introduce a pattern interrupt by being more engaging and actually making the intro portion of the video valuable, your viewers will learn to trust and enjoy the beginning of your videos versus skipping through like they usually do.

The 4 Steps to Craft a Killer Intro, especially for content-creating entrepreneurs, you need:

Step 1 | Open with a Known Tension

Step 2 | Seed for the Future Resolution

Step 3 | Showcase "The How"

Step 4 | State the Next Logical Question (N.L.Q.) but unanswered

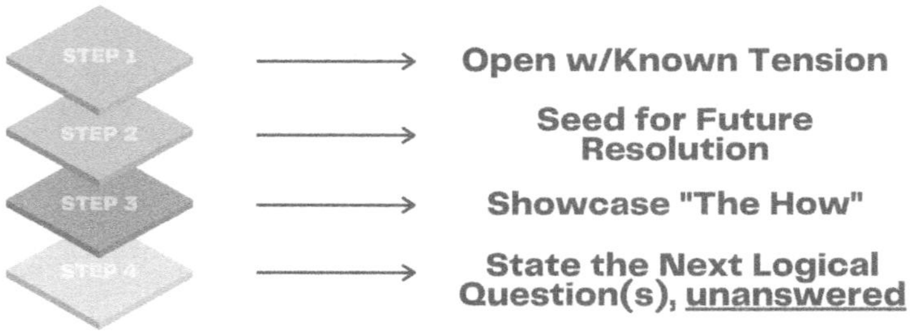

The one thing you have to keep top of mind is that regardless of how great the techniques you try to use to keep a viewer watching, they can always skip ahead to find what they're looking for. If they don't see it, they may choose to leave your video.

When originally learning YouTube and noticing viewers were leaving my videos almost immediately after clicking, I had to change how I produced my content.

Instead of trying to make them watch a 45-second or 1-2 minute intro, I simply made the decision to get to the point faster.

You can see what's happening in the beginning of your videos by selecting your video in YouTube Studio, going to the Analytics tab, then selecting Engagement and you'll see on this page your audience retention graph for that video.

You can see the exact moments when viewers became disinterested, re-engaged or even where they skipped to other sections of your video.

Here's an example of a client's audience retention graph when we first started working together.

What this graph shows is that of all the people that clicked on this video, within 20 seconds, only 19% of the viewers were still watching.

So, if 500 people clicked to watch this video initially, only 95 kept watching 20 seconds into the video.

With viewers bouncing from video to video searching for their answers, it's important to recognize you're not their video number one but their video number 100.

This is counterproductive to creating an attractive thumbnail and title that did its job, enticing them to click, only for them to skip to about the 2-minute mark or so before leaving the video.

By using the 4 Keys to a Killer Intro you can drastically change this.

Key #1 is opening with a known tension. We don't need to guess why they're clicking or what about this video is attractive to them; you're the expert. You know what they're struggling with and what they need to know to change that.

Seeding for a future resolution is giving a preview of what's to come so the viewer can judge if this video will cover what they think it will.

If the type of video you plan to create is a tutorial of some sort and similar videos range between 10-15 minutes, how likely would you be to sit up to 6-8 minutes and the video not have what you need? Not likely.

Showcasing the how is both audible and visual. You want to audibly give a very short synopsis of what you plan to cover and also show an example at that precise moment of what's to come later in the video.

Remember, there's nothing lost in showing and telling them what's to come because they can and will skip ahead if they don't have that confirmation. Keep the intros as short and concise as possible.

Stating the N.L.Q. or Next Logical Question, but unanswered, we'll cover in a bit, but know it's a way you can use to grow your email list or seed toward a future video. We'll talk more about this when breaking down the 5 Pillars for Creating Videos People Love.

The depth of the video you're creating sometimes requires a bit longer intro, but one that still captures your audience's attention and rewards them for it.

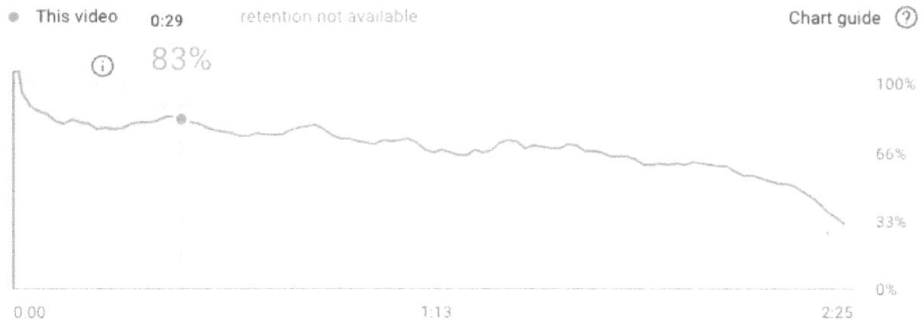

If you're a coach or consultant, here's an example of what a highly crafted intro could look like:

Step 1 | The stress of not knowing where your next coaching client will come from is very frustrating and nerve-racking.

Step 2 | Today, I'm going to share how you can keep your pipeline full of excited clients,

Step 3 | how I use this referral reference sheet to never run out of clients and,

Step 4 | I'll also share my call sheet script that earns me a 97% success rate to close my clients on the first call.

In roughly 15 seconds, you've hit every stage of this framework and can quickly transition into the main point of why your viewer clicked on the video.

You don't need a huge build-up and fanfare at the beginning of your video; create from the perspective of the person on the keyboard. When you imagine yourself as the viewer, start your video as if you're starting from an existing conversation they're already having in their mind.

The same is true even for non-profit or ministry organizations creating video content.

Step 1 | Praying can feel lonely and stressful when you're new to praying.

Step 2 | Today, I'm going to share how to pray so it doesn't feel weird & uncomfortable,

Step 3 | that praying isn't begging God for something, but the types of prayers you can use that actually work,

Step 4 | and our Scripture Reference Sheet to find helpful Bible verses to use even if you're new to reading the Bible.

See how you're able to even craft in a lead magnet that can turn viewers into community members and potential clients, which creates a richer relationship with your viewers?

If you're a marketing consultant or social media strategist, you could craft an intro covering new Instagram updates your ideal viewer would be interested in.

Step 1 | Did your Instagram reach drop by 50% this week?

Step 2 | If you're ignoring this one new IG metric, that's likely why!

Step 3 | Our brand new clients used our IG strategy and their reach jumped 87% over their best posts, and today I'm showing you how.

Step 4 | I'm also sharing how our IG DM strategy easily turn new followers into clients.

When sharing numbers and such, you want it to first be the truth.

Secondly, whenever I'm working with coaches, marketers, or finance clients, my constant reminder is to keep the numbers minimal in the intros.

People still need to be able to process what you're saying and know they want to keep watching.

Whether editing the videos yourself or hiring a video editor, you want to use the say, show, and spell method in your intros as well.

Every video has what's called the A-Roll and B-Roll in the video.

A-Roll is the primary footage (ex. you on camera) and the **B-Roll** is if you're our social media marketer sharing the video about Instagram, you'd show the screenshot of the before and after results on Instagram as you're stating them.

This is why despite all of us knowing it'll look nothing like the image on the commercial, we're still drawn to try new foods and new restaurants based on them leveraging the say, show, and spell method.

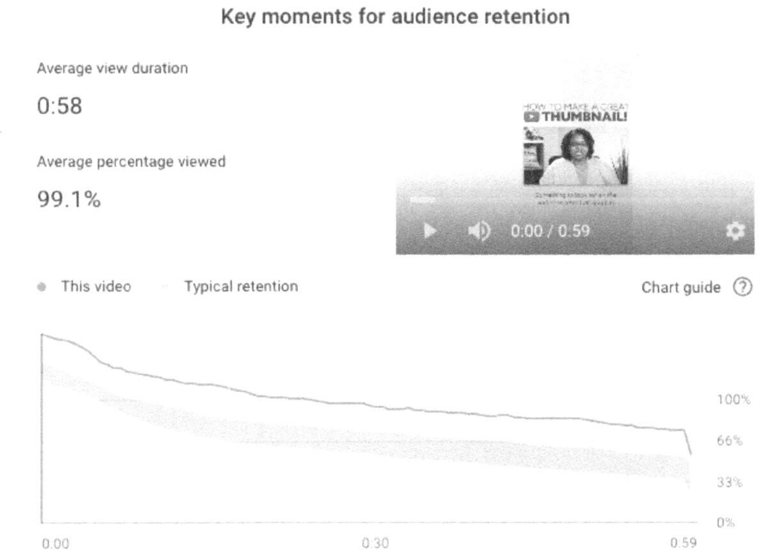

This helps keep your viewer interested, engaged, and foreshadows the solution they're desiring that you'll be covering.

When done well, a well-crafted intro can keep your viewers engaged on regular videos and even your micro-content.

The Core Content Section

With your intro sorted out, the last thing we'd want is the viewer all excited for your video and they leave disappointed with the delivery of the content.

Once you've hooked your viewer with your intro, it's now time to deliver on the rest of the video your viewer is desiring to see.

If you think about your video in blocks or sections, it's easier to not only plan your videos but record your content.

The basic video structure, or what I like to call the **Core Content Structure**. The **Core Content** is the meat and potatoes of the video; it's the reason why people clicked on the video. This format can vary depending on the type of video you'd like to create. For most education-based content creators, this format is tried and true.

It creates an easy and digestible format from which the viewer can learn and receive the information, without it feeling overloaded. In the format below, it's the content between the video intro and the next logical question.

The difference in breaking up the video in sections versus one long, unorganized monologue means the viewer can easily keep pace with what's shared or taught. This also allows the creator (you) to record your video in sections versus feeling all over the place with the delivery of your content.

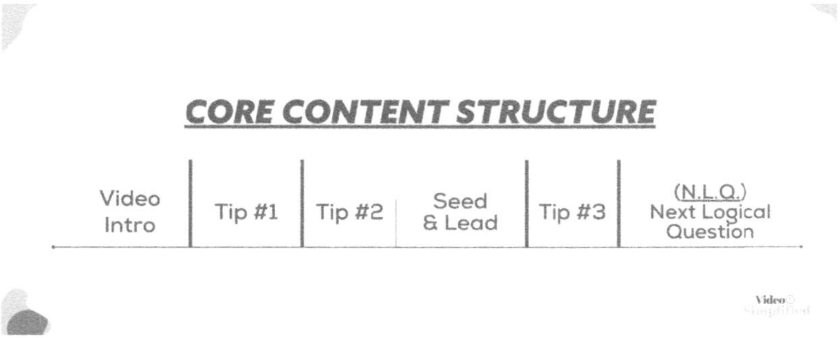

Seed & Lead

The next section of the video is the **Seed & Lead** section of the video where I'm embedding a "Pro-Tip" that provides extra bonus content in reference to the video, or I'm seeding in information the viewer would desire to know about, but we're not fully addressing in this particular video.

You may be wondering, why use the Seed & Lead method instead of adding that information as another tip to the video. The answer is simple. It's the same reason a waitress will share what special dessert they're offering that's exceptionally delicious while handing out menus: to plant the seed of dessert in your mind. You haven't even ordered your meal yet and she already has you thinking about dessert, at least for the moment.

Even as you place your order, she may bring up that special dessert again to help germinate that seed.

Then, once your meal is completed, it's time to add the cherry on top of your enjoyable meal. Could you leave the restaurant satisfied with what you've eaten? Of course. However, America isn't an overweight nation because we're all so concerned with our portion controls–we LOVE great food!

The same is true with your viewer. If the seed will lead to another video or pro-tip later down the road, no one is upset by a delicious dessert. So, seed for a future video or you can provide a pro-tip and move on to the next segment in your video.

For most education-based content, I've found the multiples of 3, 5, 7, or 10 to be the best forms of splitting up your content into digestible bits.

Despite the power of this simple format, there are times when instead of individually segmented tips, you break the content down into logically progressive steps.

For example, when I'm creating various camera and video tutorials on my YouTube channel, the "Tips" video format wouldn't be ideal.

The main question to ask yourself before planning a video is what is the best way to deliver this content for the ideal viewer?

You know your ideal viewer well, what content type would they enjoy the most?

- A Tips-Styled Video?
- A Conversational Monologue?
- A Micro-Content Delivery Style? (YouTube Shorts, TikTok, etc.)
- Vlog-Styled Content?

There will be times you step away from how you traditionally create a video to produce a piece that connects deeper than if you "presented" the information to them.

After making over 50 videos on how to get the best out of a particular camera and becoming known to teach on it, switching to another brand completely was going to be a big shift on my channel. I needed to have a conversation with my audience explaining my decision to switch brands and how that would impact the content on the channel.

So, I recorded the video in my car while running errands with my family–which was a complete shift from how I usually teach on my channel. The video was well-received and the change in scenery can help break up the monotony of always creating content in your office or studio.

There are things about your personality, interests, who you are, and what your brand stands for that should be ingrained into your content. Remember as you're creating your content to share YOU.

I love to make jokes out of my mistakes when recording, show quick bloopers, or when something is the best share if it makes the Bee's Knee's Hall of Fame awards or if I consider it to be the dark chocolate of something. Sharing fun phrases I naturally use in daily life or embedding my love of white chocolate over the horrid mud muck of a candy bar dark chocolate personalizes my content to the viewers.

I don't do it to trick viewers into liking me or use it as some "strategy," but because we're human. Human connection is what video is all about.

So, I encourage you to keep improving in your video and marketing strategies but don't forget humans love to connect with other humans. Remember to add some of who you are into your content.

CREATOR NEXT STEPS

- [ ] Consider what offer or video you'd promote using the Seed & Lead strategy.
- [ ] Use the **4 Steps to a Killer Intro** for an existing video idea you're currently working on.

Chapter 16

Creating Videos That Connects & Converts

5 Pillars for Creating Videos People Love

All viewers desire a content payoff.

Now that you know the four steps to craft intros to hook your viewers and keep them watching, it's important to make sure they experience the intended payoff they initially desired when watching your videos online.

This framework is a proven video formula that works especially well for tutorial and training-based content, to ensure you're giving your ideal viewer what they desire and omitting the things they don't. Let's expand on the video structure mentioned in the previous chapter.

Pillar #1 Get Straight to the Point

Although you may be new to video, you're likely not new to the content topics you'll cover in various videos.

Giving too much irrelevant information will cause your viewer to start skipping around in your videos, looking for the part when you finally get to why they clicked on the video. This is easily seen in audience retention graphs on YouTube when you see dips in the graph. This shows that the viewer either left the video or skipped ahead to a different part of the video.

These are known as **Key Moments**.

There are four notable types: Intros, Top Moments, Spikes, and Dips. We've covered earlier about intros and our next goal now is to avoid dips (when they leave or skip) and gradual declines where we're progressively losing people as the video advances. [3]

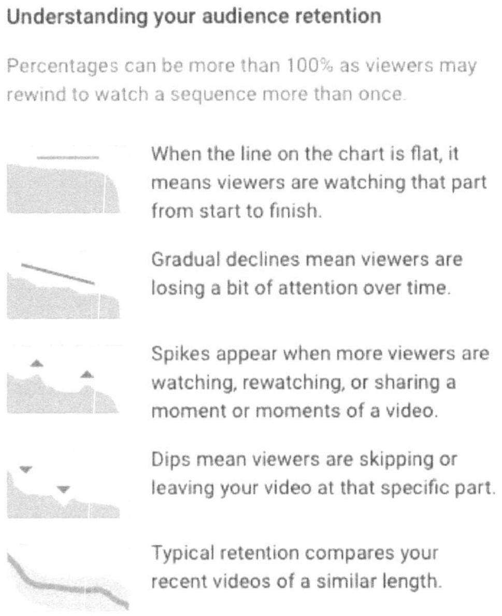

While some decrease over time is normal, we want to do all within our creative power to prevent viewers from going to another video. So, while you're in the planning phase of what video you'll create and what tips to include, be sure to only include what's relevant to the viewer's intent of why they initially clicked on the video.

Pillar #2 Open with the Viewer's Desire or Confusion Point

In the C.L.A.R.I.T.Y. Content Framework, we covered how to lead with your viewer's desire, pain point, or confusion point.

Often with instructional content even within a how-to, instructional, or update video, there is something the viewer desires and often has questions or confusion surrounding that topic. Identify what that desire is and enter the conversion already happening in your viewer's mind. Remember, the intro to your videos doesn't need to be long to convey the point. This is the hook.

Pillar #3 Core Content Breakdown

Psychologically, odd numbers are better to use in marketing content, and I've found, in video content structure. Even designers leverage the power of odd numbers in design choices to have a proper balance with design choices. For more instructional videos, breaking down the content into noticeable choices of three, five, or even seven tips, strategies, or segments gives your viewers an easily digestible format to stick with you without needing to use the cliché phrase of "stick with me."

There are times when breaking the odd number rule is helpful, and that's when sharing top 10, top 20, top 100, etc. style content. Otherwise, break up and break down your video into sections that are easier for your viewers to follow along with.

Pillar #4 Seed & Lead Method

I love the Seed & Lead Method because it's a way to introduce a future and related video. If your video covers how to import your existing warm leads into the Facebook Ads Manager system, consider what is another related or unspoken desire of your target audience.

The best way to Seed & Lead in your video is to do so naturally. You don't want to sound robotic or as if you're omitting something that actually should be included in the current video. This should be a related and separate topic, not something that might be missing from the existing video.

If using our Facebook marketer as an example, they may state it at the moment where the ads manager screen, the viewer may see where they can create a lookalike audience. Knowing your viewer's unspoken desires, you know they'll see this option on their screen and want to jump ahead. It's at this opportune moment you can seed to the viewer how valuable this option is when creating ads, but seed how you'll cover it in a bit.

This is a super powerful strategy you can leverage two ways:

- **Option 1:** Offer the reader a premium free or paid offer. This is great for PDF guides or courses you create that fully resolve the viewer's problem.

- **Option 2:** Embedded in the video to seed for a later highly desired topic.

When using option 1, be sure to actually deliver on what you promised; all viewers hate clickbait. If embedding it later in your video, use creative storytelling to keep your viewer engaged as you progress forward in your videos. Remember, this is a seed, not a meal. Briefly cover what you're seeding for and get back to the point of the video.

A simple way to implement this would be:

"If you're looking for a way to create a lookalike audience based on your warm leads list, you don't want to do that just yet. If done wrong, you'll waste a lot of money and wonder why your ads aren't converting. Later, I'll share one major overlooked strategy to make sure you're doing it the right way."

This is a great way to reinforce to your audience even more that you get them, and *you* are their go-to resource in this matter.

Converting Your Viewers

If the seed you are planting in the video is to take the viewer off the platform to your email list or a free guide, make it easy for them to connect with you.

If you've noticed throughout this book, I've shared with you ways to access various PDF downloads, a camera quiz, and more. However, these aren't via my normal website of DianaGladney.com or the traditional social media links that can become pretty lengthy.

Instead, I've linked everything to the OneRightVideo.com/ website forward slash the relevant resource's name.

Social media is the highway of attention and people are rapidly consuming content every second of the day. How will you get them to:

1. Stop the Scroll
2. Take Action on What You're Saying

This becomes increasingly easier when you make your calls to action (aka the action you want people to take in your content) very easy to remember. If the

URL you want them to type in looks like website coding, the conversion rate will be horrible. It needs to be easy for people to follow through.

Even if you don't have a dedicated website yet, you can use tools like ReBrandly to create redirect links to whatever products or services you're using. I specifically covered time-saving techniques in the beginning of this book because we're all busy with something. If someone desires what you're offering, make it easy for them to do business with you.

This also helps me keep track of where someone is coming from when finding my content. For example, OneRightVideo.com/YouTube and Diana.Link/Y ouTube will both take you to my YouTube channel.

However, if I only share the link using the book URL in this book, I know you came from certain chapters in this book. Whereas the other link, I would know they're coming from TikTok or another app.

This is great for those of us that love to see the data and analytics of our creative efforts and dedicated link tracking helps to do that.

Some great options to create memorable links are:

- Purchasing a Dedicated URL to Use
- ReBrandly
- Pretty Link (WordPress website plugin)
- Bit.ly
- Geniuslink

As of the time I'm writing this book, YouTube does not offer any direct messaging services. So, Instagram DM-type strategies aren't possible on YouTube currently. So, make it as few clicks as possible for people to either checkout and purchase what you're offering.

YouTube's expansion of features like the Community Tab also make it possible to share images, GIFs, links to videos, polls, etc. with clickable links. When you've gone through the effort of seeding in and adding various C.T.A.s in your videos, double down on that and share a secondary or reminder piece via the Community Tab.

Seeding content can become even more strategic when you know you've planned a live video that's starting soon or planning to release a specific video. I like to go into my YouTube Studio and start catching up on responding to subscriber comments. Those that can be addressed, or will be, in a live or recorded video, will be communicated in the comment as well.

This type of **engagement driving** brings the viewer back to either your video or the YouTube app via notification due to the replied comment they've just received and also links to a video, upcoming live stream, or a recommended product or service.

I love doing this before a live stream because it greatly increases the chances of that particular person coming to the live stream and I have the opportunity to connect and engage with them directly.

Remember, videos are about creating connections; humans connecting with other humans.

Pillar #5: Next Logical Question & Call to Action

This is nearing the end of the video and where most entrepreneurs and marketers drop the ball. In normal life conversation, it seems normal to say goodbye, but that shouldn't be the case in videos. Instead of treating your videos like a phone call, treat them like a text message. Text messages don't end, and we don't say goodbye.

At best, we say we'll check back in and talk with that person later. In video, we want to keep the conversation going by directing them to the next conversation, aka your video.

Think of the ending of your video as another form of intro. It's crafted almost in the same format, but when you're nearing the end of your final tip, weave in the next logical question technique. The N.L.Q. is all about thinking through, what's the next logical question the viewer would ask themselves after watching this video? The N.L.Q. is easiest to execute when you know your target audience's customer journey.

Here are some examples:

— If sharing how to forgive yourself as a life coach, the next logical question could be how to take better ownership of your mistakes, vs letting them continuously crush you.

— If writing how to create a Facebook ad, the next logical question could be common mistakes to avoid.

— If you're a copywriter making videos about email copy, the next logical question could identify why your open rate is so low.

The next logical question is built around knowing your target audience's desires, frustrations, and future steps. Sometimes they're taking steps out of order, so it's guiding them back to the video they should have watched first. Once you've identified what the next logical question is, the C.T.A. or Call to Action becomes easier.

You can lead them to a free download, book a call for the next steps, or as simple as going to the next video that's the most logical progression in their customer journey.

Remember, your videos should be a pain reliever for them. This structure allows you to do that as you become a content-creating entrepreneur.

CREATOR NEXT STEPS

- [ ] Review your existing videos or planned videos, and make sure they follow the **5 Pillars for Creating Videos People Love**.
- [ ] What's the **Next Logical Question** your audience is silently wondering when completing your video?

Chapter 17

My Secret Sauce for Every Video

As entrepreneurs, many would consider our educational content as boring, and mostly, they'd be correct...mostly.

However, this is where you get to add some spice and variety to the type of content you'll be creating.

Remember, this book is a guidebook that will give you the fundamental structures I've found to universally work, no matter your niche or industry, but as with all recipes, don't feel restricted from adding in your own unique flavor and styles to the content structures shared in this book.

Who Are You Creating This Video For?

This is the starting point of any video you create for your business. If you already own a business where you offer a service or a product, chances are you are already aware of who your ideal customer is. When creating video content, you want to take a similar approach by first identifying your ideal viewer.

When I worked with a client who owned a coaching business, I asked him, "Who is your ideal viewer? Who is the person that will get the greatest benefit from watching this video?"

He confidently replied, "Well, everyone! Anybody who watches this video will get value from it."

I explained to him that this couldn't be further from the truth. When "everyone" is the target audience, no one will truly resonate with the video. One of my favorite ways to explain the concept of identifying your content niche on YouTube for entrepreneurs is that your content should always be attracting and repelling someone.

When I create camera tutorials on how to use certain models or what certain camera settings mean, I intentionally state who the video is for and who it's not for. If someone wants to become a better filmmaker or photographer, they may still learn something by hearing a simplified camera explanation. However, the video is intentionally created for content-creating entrepreneurs getting started in video that has no intention of becoming a professional filmmaker.

Instead, the entrepreneur's interest is learning to create better videos for their brand and business. While another YouTube video may cover the exact same camera, our ideal viewers have very different desired outcomes.

Whether it's avoiding certain jargon or choosing to use specific industry terms, you instantly segment the viewership of your videos; this isn't a bad thing. Imagine being frustrated needing to make a change on your smartphone and every video generically says "iPhone" or "Android." How frustrated would you be that you couldn't locate the specific year and model you needed help with? This is how audiences feel when they can't find videos specifically addressing their desired point of confusion or frustration.

By identifying the ideal viewer and serving the one person you have in mind, you easily become the go-to resource for many of your ideal viewers fitting that description.

The C.L.A.R.I.T.Y. Content Framework™

Creating videos people are interested in, receive real tangible value from, and love is the magic behind building a channel, and brand subscribers keep coming back to and new viewers feel like they've struck gold when they find your channel.

Comments like,

— "Your approach is definitely a stand-out approach. I don't feel 'less intelligent,' or 'confused' after watching your videos. I feel like... 'oh...I might be able to pull this off myself if I dedicate the time and have the right mindset.' So, thank you for that."

— "The BEST video I've come across that explains the exposure triangle. I finally GET it! Wow! Thank you so much for explaining this in such a simple language. I feel like I just won the lottery. This will save me so much time with trying to get my settings right every time. Thank you, Diana! You are the absolute BEST!!"

— "I found your channel a week ago, and all I can say is that you're inspirational. I'm just getting started and videos like yours keep me focused and informed. Thanks for taking the time to put together content we can all use and digest. I want to be like you when my channel grows up :)"

— "I'm so glad I found your channel!!!! I've binge-watched all your videos, and it feels like a community!!!"

— "Hey, Diana, just found your channel and am literally binge-watching everything. Thank you for the clear and concise content..."

— "You have no idea how helpful this was for me. Thank you so much. Now to binge the rest of your videos. Thank you."

These, along with literally thousands of others, are the types of comments I get on my channel daily because of how I structure my videos, and how they're broken down to best serve my target audience.

These are the types of comments your channel can receive when you learn to upload content that connects and converts your audience.

The framework I'm about to share with you is the exact framework I still use to this day to make sure when I'm planning and scripting my videos. I make sure by the time I get to the end of my video, I know it will accomplish the task I set for that video, and yours can too.

To Connect with Your Audience, Your Message Must Be Clear

The C.L.A.R.I.T.Y. Content Framework is an acronym to help when reviewing your content to make sure your videos do their job. Use this framework as a filter to strain out any fluff and to avoid overstuffing your videos with things that diminish the value to the viewer.

As one of my mentors, Heather Torres, taught me, it's better to be clear than clever. This is what each letter of the C.L.A.R.I.T.Y. Content Framework stands for:

C | Confusion Point

L | Lay It Out

A | Articulate the Problem

R | Relieve the Pain Point/Issue

I | Interest/Insight/Inspiration

T | Transformation

Y | Yes? Can You Answer *Yes* to This Question?

When I first started working with Heather Torres years ago, I remember from our very first call, she kept telling me to make sure my messaging was clear. She'd ask me, "Diana, is your content easy to understand or is it too complex that they'd be confused?"

Especially working with entrepreneurs who are looking to transition into video content creation, it is important to realize they aren't trying to become a photographer, and they aren't interested in becoming a filmmaker—so how can I teach and share concepts they can easily understand and digest?

Over and over, she drilled into my head to make sure my messaging was clear.

When working with my other mentor, Ray Edwards, he drilled the importance of making sure your copy does its job. Ray teaches copywriters how to write the words that sell with his P.A.S.T.O.R. Copywriting Framework and that is what inspired me to create my framework that followed the same system I implemented in my video creation process, but in a duplicatable system I could teach for video. When I shared this framework with him, I was honored when his first response to hearing it was "Brilliant!"

I'm going to break down and share with you this C.L.A.R.I.T.Y. Content Framework that'll ensure by the time you're done crafting and creating a video, you're confident it does the job you intended, and is clear and easy to understand, without overstuffing your videos with information it shouldn't include.

"C" | Confusion Point

As entrepreneurs, all of our businesses were formed by solving a problem. Creating video content is no different.

The "C" in the C.L.A.R.I.T.Y. Content Framework is starting with the primary point of confusion for your target audience that your video is going to address.

What are they most frustrated about and what is annoying them the most about this problem? This is where we begin our videos each and every time.

The social behavior of viewers on YouTube usually begins with them having a problem and searching for an answer.

To make sure my videos were hitting the nail on the head, I needed to make sure they cut through the fluff and frustrations most viewers would have. Based on their right-now pain point that's causing them to search for a solution to this issue online, what are some common issues this viewer is encountering?

I always teach that you're not your viewer's video number 1; you're often their video number 100. Chances are they've seen other videos before yours, read blog posts, or generated their questions based on the problem they're trying to solve.

When we begin our videos by addressing what may confuse the viewer, we can begin to instantly connect with them in a way no other video may be doing online.

For a realtor creating videos for a first-time home buyer, the viewer may be confused between the first-time home buyer loan and the first-time home buyer program in a specific state.

By beginning your videos with the Confusion Point of the viewer, based on the video's topic you're covering, you are beginning to speak to what I consider addressing the elephant in the room right away.

For a business coach, you may address common mindset issues your potential clients have and create a video about having a true limitation that needs to be addressed versus having the viewers come to grips with the reality. They may just be afraid and need to address that fear head-on.

I did this with a post on TikTok that quickly shot to 20k views because I addressed a common issue that comes up with those just getting started in video. New creators always complain about having consistency issues. When the truth is, they're just afraid.

I started the video with the confusion point and by addressing the big elephant in the room that everyone tiptoes around, by saying,

"You don't have consistency issues. Either you don't care or you're just not committed to what you're doing."

This opened up the comments section to allow a lot of people to finally be honest and transparent with themselves by admitting they actually were afraid and asking for help to address those fears.

This made the viewers finally address the root issue: Do they really care about what they're wanting to create videos around, or is building a YouTube channel not really a priority.

When you start with the elephant in the room and address what may be confusing or frustrating the viewer, you instantly capture their attention and can keep it for much longer than videos that don't.

"L" | Lay It All Out

How many times have you ever clicked on a YouTube video, and you have to keep scanning through the video to see if this person has your answer or not? Think of how frustrating that is when you're the viewer, and keep that in mind when creating your content.

Don't romanticize the content you're creating and assume, because you're "the expert," that the viewer should just automatically listen to you.

You're not the expert to them yet. When they first click on your video, you're just an option among hundreds and thousands of other videos they could watch on your topic. So, get to the point.

To lay it all out for the viewer, answer the following:

1. What are they going to learn?

2. What are you going to cover and resolve in this video?

When you lay out all you plan to cover or what you're not going to cover in the beginning of your video, it instantly lets your viewers know if this is the right video for them or not.

At the beginning of your video, lay out what you plan to cover by saying something like:

"In this video, I'm going to share how to {Resolve Problem #1}, so that you can {Desired End-Result Goal} by {How you plan to address the issue}."

This may sound like "you're giving away the goods upfront," because you are. This works so much better than asking a viewer to "stick around" for a hopeful answer instead of letting them know you know what their pain point is, you plan to address it, and here's how.

This locks your viewer in to watch the rest of the video because they quickly can recognize *you* have their solution.

"A" | Articulate the Problem

If you've addressed the elephant in the room and laid out what you plan to cover, you may wonder what else there is to talk about at the beginning of the video.

When you articulate the problem, this allows you time to review and refine the wording in your video's intro to optimize it for audience retention (keeping the viewers watching).

Ask yourself:

1. What is the real underlying issue the viewer is having?

2. What's causing the confusion or miscommunication?

Make sure that you've articulated the problem well by speaking the viewers' language in a way they'd actually understand and resonate with.

This is how you get comments like I literally just got the day before writing this chapter of the book, where a viewer stated:

"Thank you! I was so confused because I'm not getting much blur with the kit lens. I'm shooting indoors (and totally new to photography/videography). Thanks for explaining!"

Or comments like,

"THIS IS SO GOOD!! Finally a video that really goes deeper with logical tools + actionable steps."

When you're too busy being "the expert," you often overlook the value of addressing your audience's primary confusion points in their language, not yours.

I worked with an accounting client that helped business owners get out of their financial pitfalls by clarifying what areas to pay attention to when reviewing their finances and how to take control of their finances when they're on the verge of financial ruin.

While helping him plan out his videos and how to research topics and vet his video ideas, while listening to him read off the video ideas he had in mind, I asked him, "Does your target audience actually understand that language you're using yet, or would they be further confused by what you're saying?"

The look on his face gave me the answer to that question long before he verbalized, "No, they wouldn't know that language yet."

When you're articulating the problem the viewer is facing, the goal is not to use industry jargon they may not understand yet, but by using the language from the perspective of the viewer searching for answers on the keyboard.

"R" | Relieve Their Pain Point/Issue

The "R" is the delivery process you'll take to deliver the solution to the viewer.

Ask yourself:

1. What's the best way to deliver their relief?

2. Which video format would serve them best? (Tips, tutorials, in-depth strategies, how-to, a vlog-style video, live stream, reaction-style video, etc.)

There are multiple video format styles you can use to share the content of your video. If you were like a doctor, based on what is confusing the viewer, ask yourself which video format style is the best way to deliver this medicine.

If someone has a toothache, the last thing they'd want is to be administered medicine that has to be chewed for it to work - they'd never be able to get through it.

The same is true with education-based content. Consider the ways you can potentially address the pain point of your viewer, and which video format would be the best way to relieve their issues.

When I'm covering various cameras that have just been released, oftentimes, my target audience likely doesn't know the first thing about this camera or how to set it up to get to a place they can even begin to record a video. Knowing this, some of the first videos I'll create for a new camera is how to set it up and optimize it for video.

This video isn't best served as a "Tips" style video because it'd leave too many gaps unaddressed in that style of video. In that case, an in-depth how-to video is usually my go-to. These are longer-form videos, but it ensures by the time the viewer is done with the video, they've been well-served, and their primary pain point has been addressed.

This leads to comments like:

"This video was so helpful. Thank you for taking time to break everything down for us newbies!! You gained a new sub!"

or

"What a great video! Arguably, one of the most thorough out there on this camera. Plus, you took the time to explain, give context and offered places to go that expand on various aspects of the settings. Spot on...and well done! :-)"

How you choose to deliver your content can be the difference in relieving your viewers' pain points or creating one for them.

"I" | Interest, Insight, or Inspiration

The "I" is the intersection of the pain point and the solution. People search for and watch YouTube videos based on their interests, looking to gain new insight or inspiration from the content.

This doesn't exclude making your content entertaining, but we'll dive more into that in Chapter 18 on "Overlooked Secrets of Storytelling."

Ask yourself:

1. Where are other videos on this topic missing the mark?

Yes, you guessed it, when you're researching content on your video's topic, you should go and look at what are fellow creators in your niche covering or not covering in their videos.

This isn't about "beating the competition," but rather getting a better understanding of what your viewer is struggling with, what's frustrating them the most, and how you can best help them.

Based on your video topic, is this something that's of interest to them, something they're trying to gain more insight on, like how to do something better, or is it something that will inspire them to take action on something?

You can create much deeper connections when the solutions to your viewer's questions truly dive deeper into why they care about this issue so much or what they want to get out of it. It goes far beyond tips or tutorial videos to why they're actually researching the issues and what they truly want.

Review the comments on your existing videos and other videos, blog posts, or even tweets on similar topics to your video to see how your viewers truly feel and what they think.

You can now use this information to your advantage to truly inspire, capture and keep their attention by seeing what other creators may have omitted, missed or overlooked, or even created a video with the assumption the audience understands a concept when, in reality, they do not.

The comments section will always tell you what was missing and overlooked from the viewer's perspective. Armed with this information, it becomes like a homing beacon to further align the solution you're providing with the expectations of the viewer.

"T" | Transformational Value

The "T" is about creating Transformational Value for the viewer.

Ask yourself:

1. What's the transformation that's taking place for the viewer because of this video?

2. What does watching this video make possible for them?

Sometimes it's hard to see the value in a simple tutorial video, especially for businesses and brands. Later, in Chapter 18, we'll cover how the videos you create, even simple tutorials, play a vital role for your target audience, and why they will connect and resonate with your videos over others.

This couldn't be further from the truth because your videos aren't just a simple A-B, Solution, and Problem concepts. When I'm sharing how to use a camera or a YouTube tutorial, the purpose of the video has to go beyond just setting up a camera, to realizing I'm helping creators get over the hurdle and frustration of using this camera that will help be the catalyst for them, not only changing someone else's life but changing their own lives as well.

Watching content and reading books from my mentors and coaches went far beyond just that basic tutorial, but empowered me to change my life.

When you answer what this video makes possible for your target audience and what transformational value it possesses for them, you begin to answer the vital question my friend Jeff Barsch posed of "What's the thing under the thing?"

Sharing with a first-time home buyer what they need to be approved for their first home isn't just about answering that basic question, but empowering them to provide a safe and loving home to start a family. Or to finally go from living on a family member's sofa or basement to finally getting a home they can call their own.

This is what Jeff calls "the thing under the thing" and what creates Transformational Value to the viewer.

How is the video you're creating going to create transformational value for the viewer?

"Y" | Yes? Can You Answer Yes to the Following Question?

The "Y" is being able to answer *Yes* to the following question:

Can the viewer leave this video with the **intended transformation**? Or do they need to watch something or someone else's content after yours to get that transformation?

When you're able to answer yes to this question, you will undoubtedly know that your video has achieved the purpose you set out for it to achieve.

When you process your videos through the C.L.A.R.I.T.Y. Content Framework, you should be able to answer *Yes* that your video will be successful in providing the intended transformation your viewer initially desired when searching for an answer to the problem your video addresses.

If you cannot answer *Yes*, then it will help you identify what your video is missing, what to add in or what to take out to keep the central focus on the primary intended transformation.

C.L.A.R.I.T.Y. Content Framework Recap

C | Confusion Point

L | Lay It Out

A | Articulate the Problem

R | Relieve the Pain Point/Issue

I | Interest/Insight/Inspiration

T | Transformation

Y | Yes? Can You Answer *Yes* to This Question?

There are two places in your video creation process you should use the C.L.A .R.I.T.Y. Content Framework in your workflow:

1. When you're scripting and planning your videos.

and

2. When you're reviewing the edited version of your video (or during the editing process, if editing yourself).

The reason you want to review it during the planning process is to ensure you're including all the right elements of your videos.

When reviewing it during the editing/reviewing process, you can watch the semifinished version and make sure you didn't ad-lib too much additional content that, in hindsight, is now bloating the video and causing it to have too much fluff in the content.

You'd be surprised how giving your video a second look through the C.L.A.R .I.T.Y. Content Framework filter will help enrich the quality of your videos.

CREATOR NEXT STEPS

- [ ] Filter your video through the **C.L.A.R.I.T.Y. Content Framework™** while planning and during the editing process.

C.L.A.R.I.T.Y. Content Framework™ Recap

C Confusion Point

L Lay It Out

A Articulate the Problem

R Relieve the Pain Point/Issue

I Interest/Insight/Inspiration

T Transformation

Y Yes? Can You Answer Yes to This Question?

Chapter 18

Overlooked Secrets of Storytelling

It doesn't take watching too many videos on YouTube on becoming a content creator before you hear endless tips on how vital storytelling is to video content creation.

That sounds great for filmmakers and possibly other entertainment-based content niches, but for entrepreneurs, it can be hard to see how storytelling can be embedded into business content.

I remember initially struggling with this concept, trying to see how storytelling could be used in videos about cameras and live-streaming software. It didn't make any sense.

Somewhere in my journey, I was introduced to the book by Donald Miller, *Building A Story Brand*. This was the answer to making the connection of storytelling for business owners.

In his book, he exposes the 7-Step Story Brand Framework of how to implement storytelling in your business.

He says every story is generally framed as,

"A CHARACTER who wants something encounters a PROBLEM before they can get it. At the peak of their despair, a GUIDE steps into their lives, gives them a PLAN, and CALLS THEM TO ACTION. That action helps them avoid FAILURE and ends in a SUCCESS." [4]

The most important aspect of this storytelling framework is understanding, as the content creator, we are not the hero in this story; we are the guide.

When creating your content, if you remember that your role in this character's journey (the viewer) is to be their Yoda, you can better understand how your videos play a role in helping them execute the calls to action you give them that helps them avoid failure and ends in a success.

Infusing Storytelling Into Education-Based Content

You may ask, how can this apply to simple education-based content. *Easily.*

Suppose a mom's been struggling with detangling her four-year-old's hair for weeks on end. She's at her wits end trying to avoid hurting her daughter's head but styling her hair in a way that's manageable no matter what destruction her kid gets into.

This is the starting point of our hero's journey. If you own or are recommending a specific detangling product for kids, it's at this moment where your content and your video's problem intersect.

1. **A Character:** A mom
2. **Who Has a Problem**: Wants to detangle and style her rambunctious four-year-old's hair without hurting her and stressing out trying to always manage it.
3. **Who Meets a Guide**: You and your product or service.
4. **Who Gives Them a Plan**: How to use or solve this mom's detangling

and styling woes with her daughter.

5. **And Calls Them to Action**: Teaching this mom how to easily style and detangle hair by providing additional style options that are kid destruction proof.

6. **That Ends in a Success**: Solves this mom's pain point of constantly fighting to keep her kid's hair healthy and in kid destruction-proof styles.

7. **That Helps Them Avoid Failure**: Prevents mom from reliving the daily dread of picking her kid up from school to see her hair looks nothing like the style she formed that morning and back to the tangled mess she'd just conquered that morning.

Do you see how storytelling has nothing to do with the video creator, but focuses the main attention on helping the hero have a successful resolution to their right-now pain point?

Storytelling Content Types

There are several video types and locations you can leverage as a video creator that can re-engage your audience's leveraging storytelling. You can create these videos completely using these different video types or embed segments that can break up the monotony of your typical business videos. Here are some video types and locations that can help give a fresh spin and introduce new storytelling elements.

You can record content:

1. While vlogging

2. At a park or outdoor location

3. In your hotel or Airbnb

4. In your car
5. While traveling
6. Waiting for a flight
7. At a park or outdoor location
8. In an Uber or Lyft
9. At church
10. Outside/Inside a rental property
11. In your home office
12. While visiting a colleague
13. By creating multiple recording locations in your office
14. At an event/conference
15. Embedding interview content
16. Sharing recorded talks or presentations
17. Asking a fellow creator to share a video tip or collaborate
18. When taking a walk

When you understand how your videos play a part in your customer's journey, you can alter the words you use or the examples you give to start getting comments like those I see on my channel stating:

"Oh my, it's like you are reading my mind. I was struggling with that in this morning's livestream."

or

"It's like you're reading my mind."

and

"Thanks, Diana, you have been reading my mind..." By crafting your videos from the perspective of the person on the keyboard, and how your video plays a vital role in the journey, you can better season and craft your videos using these storytelling elements that connect deeper with your audience. There are lots of books on storytelling, but by far, Donald Miller's *Building a Story Brand* book is the best way to bridge the gap between learning how to connect your message with your viewer's pain point, and leveraging storytelling, to turn viewers into customers.

To get the full breakdown of the 7-Step Story Brand Framework, I highly encourage you to read *Building a Story Brand*.

CREATOR NEXT STEPS

- ☐ How can you infuse storytelling techniques covered in this chapter in your next video?
- ☐ Check out *Building a Story Brand* by Donald Miller here: **OneRightVideo.com/StoryBrandBook**

Chapter 19

The Secret to Hiring a Dope Video Editor

As a business owner, you're creating your videos to amplify your business and your brand, not become a filmmaker or videographer.

The goal of learning video is to wear a thousand hats all at once. In the beginning, you're identifying how you want to craft your videos and if YouTube and creating video content is even right for you.

Once you've identified that video content creation is right for your brand, it's easy to recognize how time-consuming planning, recording, and editing your videos can become. Especially when you're already a busy entrepreneur.

This is when it's time to remove one of the hats you've been trying to wear and manage, and hire a video editor so all you have to do is sit down, record your content and forward the videos to your editor to transform them into awesome videos for your brand.

If you're starting off as a solopreneur, and you haven't built a team yet, this can be daunting.

- How do you choose a great video editor that really understands your brand?

- How do you avoid getting ripped off while working remotely?

Let's dive into how you can begin hiring a video editor to regain your time and remove the stress of editing your videos and ten of my favorite questions to ask during an interview to sift through the chaff when hiring an editor.

The First Step to Hiring a Video Editor

How well you're organized *before* hiring a video editor, the easier the process becomes to onboard and have a video editor be able to easily transition into editing your videos.

There are 3 Phases to Hiring a Video Editor:

— **Phase 1** | The Pre-Hire Phase, What to Do Before You Hire

— **Phase 2** | The Application, Interview & Hiring Process

— **Phase 3** | Defining Your Brand's Culture & Team Building

Begin with identifying what you actually need help with the most, when you plan to start hiring (set a date), and building a structure to onboard your new team member.

If you've never hired a video editor, let's start with getting you organized and prepped for your editor to begin working.

When you begin with the end in mind, you can structure your systems for working with your video editor to be easy and seamless. If you hire a video editor, and they begin working for you, and it's a confusing, jumbled mess, they're going to quickly get frustrated and quit.

Efficiently Organizing & Structuring Your Content

Here's the organizational structure I use with Dropbox to keep my content organized, so it's easy for my video editors to work.

You'll want to do this before you hire your video editor.

Folder Structure Layout

Our team uses a numbered Dropbox Folder Structure, so folders don't reorganize when new folders are added.

- **0. Creator Brand Assets** (This includes items like your brand assets (logos, branding kit, software editing plugins, etc.))
- **1. Your Name YouTube Videos**
    - **1a.** Raw Files for YouTube Videos
    - **1b.** YouTube Thumbnails (if you choose to save them)
    - **1c.** Final & Approved YouTube Videos (if you choose to save them)
- **2. Social Media Micro-Content Main Folder**
    - **2a.** Images
    - **2b.** Videos
    - **2c.** Audio
- **3. Your Podcast Folder** (if you have one)
    - **3a.** Podcast Assets

    - **3b.** Final Podcast Episodes (if you save them)

- **4. Video Review Process**
    - Where videos are uploaded for review by your video editor.
- **5. Courses, Training, or Freemium Offers**
    - **5a.** Course Name Main Folder
        - **5a-1.** Course Name Assets
        - **5a-2.** Course Name Images
        - **5a-3.** Course Name PDFs, Guides, etc.

By creating a simple and easy-to-use folder structure, it becomes far easier for a new video editor to get started and find anything they'd need for your brand.

Most entrepreneurs are terrible with digital storage organization, but it's essential to avoid having to "quickly go look" for this PDF or where that video is saved.

Outsourcing Do's & Don'ts (to Avoid Getting Ripped Off)

You can hire locally in your country or state if you prefer, or hire overseas video editors to outsource the editing. Both have their advantages, but hiring overseas can often be much more cost-effective when starting as a solopreneur.

For this book, I'll be focusing on hiring an overseas remote video editor versus hiring locally, but the same principles still apply.

1. The Application Process

To craft an application that sifts through those that are blindly copying and pasting a generic "dear sir or madam" application, I embed elements that are required for their application to be reviewed.

If the application is not filled out properly with those elements, I note on the application post that their application will be automatically deleted.

This may seem a bit harsh initially, but when I put out a job post, I receive literally hundreds of applications for those applying for the position. To avoid spending hours at a time sifting through applications, I format my application to make sure it only includes the essentials I need to see if someone meets the basic requirements or not.

Specifying that they *must* use a professional video editing software like Final Cut Pro, Adobe Premiere Pro or Davinci Resolve instantly cuts out brand new video editors using programs like Wondershare Filmora.

While Filmora is very capable, it can't adapt to our existing video plugins and tools used to create content in the business.

Another great sifting option to add to a video job post is for them to share their internet speeds when connected via Wi-Fi only and ethernet connections only.

If their internet speeds are abysmal, there's no way we can work together because it'd take them literally days to download the large 4k video files we use when producing content. Let alone 10-bit video footage for newer high-quality cameras.

When outlining what elements you want to add to your job opening, consider what elements you'd value in a video editor, like their editing turnaround time (how long it takes them to edit a video), how creative they are when working with education-based content, and so forth.

I always ask to see certain types of videos for review, versus me wasting time sifting through an assortment of videos that may not be relevant to the kind of content they'll be editing in this role.

If hiring a video editor for vlogging, ask to see only examples of their work that is specifically vlog-style content. If you're looking to teach specific ministry education-based videos, ask to see video examples of other non-profits or educational videos they've edited before.

If someone only edits social media ads, they likely wouldn't be an ideal match for editing vlog-style content, etc. So, vet your applicants well.

2. The Interview Process

When interviewing potential candidates for your video editors, do it via video conferencing calls vs. emails or messages only.

I want to see how great of a connection I actually have with someone to see if it might be a good fit or not. I've spoken with candidates via emails before and thought they'd be a great fit, then when speaking in person, it's a complete 180° difference that ends up not being a great fit.

In my course, Building a Team, I share the best 17 interview questions to ask whether you're hiring a video editor or a virtual assistant for your brand.

Some of those questions include:

1. Have they ever worked with a foreign employer before?

- If they haven't, they may not be aware of how to actually work with you or what that process would be like.

2. Are they able to handle large 4k video editing files?

- How they answer this question will give me insights into how well they work with large files if there are any potential editing or computer issues they've run into with previous clients or not.

- If they say yes, but nearly all of their previous clients only sent 1080p video files, this person may not fully understand I'm not talking about four-minute 4k video files, but 20-, 30-, and 45-minute trainings at times that need to be edited in the business.

A response like this would prompt me to ask a follow-up question like what's the average file size their previous clients have sent over for editing and what's the largest video file size they've ever received.

If they give me a response like 5 GB files or 12 GB files, in my world, that's super small files. Some of our 4k social media-micro content files are that size. So, this likely tells me this person may not be able to handle the max workload when working with long-form training files, etc.

3. Onboarding New Team Members

This is the make-or-break part of the process that can overwhelm or delight a new team member. If you give them access to your cloud storage system, and it looks like an explosion happened with images, videos, and documents all over the place, you're going to set the wrong tone for your new team member.

My brain operates on systems and efficiencies, so I love a well-organized process on how to complete various tasks in the business. I love knowing exactly where to go when looking for specific files.

I recommend creating a dedicated team folder for all of your content, as shown previously, so you can share with your editor where everything is located for them to begin working.

If they have to keep constantly stopping to ask you "where's this or that," it's going to take them forever to edit a simple video. Consider the type of work you'll need your video editor to complete, what, if any, trainings would be involved, and what training content you might need to provide to onboard them into learning the ropes of your brand or business.

If your goal is to reclaim your time to re-focus back on your brand, I'd highly encourage you to hire a video editor for your content.

If the idea of hiring remotely makes you nervous and you're unsure of how to even begin to approach doing this for video, these are the exact methods I use in the Building a Team course. From protecting your digital assets, how to avoid getting ripped off, and all the swipe files and systems used in my business from hiring to performing daily tasks.

You can access the course here at: http://BuildingATeam.Live

Creative Editing

There will come a point in your content creation journey where you become slightly bored with the content you're creating, have a desire to explore producing your content differently, or just want to improve the way your content is performing online to keep your audience engaged and excited as you release new videos over the years.

Regardless of the reason, the desire to constantly improve the quality of your content is a factor in every content creator's journey. With the introduction of new ideas comes the time to also improve the editing, pacing, and storytelling capabilities of your content, which I believe can be greatly helped with introducing creative editing.

Creative editing is the concept of introducing a type of rebrand to your show's production by adding in new segments, new and interesting elements, or more engaging ways to tell the same information, but in a different way than you've previously shared on your YouTube channel.

For entrepreneurs, it can be difficult to find new and creative ways to do this without feeling as if you're operating disingenuously to your true character and nature. However, as a 99.987% introvert, allow me to tell you, that's good for you! When embracing the discomfort that a new idea might feel weird, silly, or just too different, I encourage you to lean into that a bit more and adopt the idea to introduce creative editing into your content.

Most education-based videos have a traditional style flow of A + B + C = D. This could be an accountant making a tutorial video sharing to get the result of "D" with a simple linear delivery style of the content. However, by leveraging storytelling, you can easily infuse the same information into a different delivery format that creates more pattern interrupts for your viewers that keep their attention.

For our accountant creator, she can use storytelling by changing her video introduction style from:

"If you're having {problem A} that's causing {problem B}, today, I'm going to share my three tips to help you get {solution D}."

What's wrong with this content style?

Nothing, honestly; even I use this linear delivery style often. However, over the course of creating videos for years, even *you* will become bored with the way you are presenting certain pieces of content and want to "switch it up" to express those same tips differently. Let's reuse the example from our accountant friend and see how she can leverage some storytelling into her content style.

Likely, our accountant friend, let's call her Sara, has a few clients she's working with already that are experiencing this very same issue she's going to teach in her video. However, instead of just sharing the tips in a bland video, let's craft a story of a client suffering from the problems that Sara's solutions can solve and create a video leveraging creative storytelling.

Let's recap from Chapter 18 the basic storytelling framework.

It's about a character who wants something, goes on a journey to get it, encounters a guide who gives them a plan that leads them to success to avoid failure, and the character is forever changed by it. However, when it comes to visual storytelling, how we begin our videos is the crux of capturing attention to draw the viewer in and make them care to keep watching.

Following this storytelling structure, let's leverage a client's actual story to introduce Sara's solution, but with a catch: we're not going to only tell this story; we're going to show it.

If Sara's original video idea was how to identify where the leaks are in your finances by dissecting your financial reports, this could be a simple video she makes in her home office. However, instead of that, we're going to leverage one of Sara's local clients who own a coffee shop and is losing money faster than they can make it and are unsure why it's happening.

Sara agrees to take a day out of her schedule to spend with this client to give them her undivided attention, assess how this business is operating, and then later sit down with her client to discuss the accounting books and where she sees they need to make changes.

We can introduce this video to Sara's YouTube community with a better introduction that could start like this:

A Clip from Sara's Client: "If we keep operating at this rate, I'll be shutting down my shop by the end of the year."

The video then shows some moments of tension in the video from this day shared at Sara's client's shop with a clip that ends with one of Sara's concerns voiced while secretly monitoring the shop that says something like:

A Clip from Sara: "I didn't know things were this bad off. I thought she was exaggerating when we first talked on the phone, but this is worse than I thought. If I can't figure this out fast, this business is closing."

We end this intro with a voice-over from Sara, stating:

"I'm taking a full day to assess one of my clients who is concerned they're losing money at a rapid rate and have to find the gaps or their shop might be closing for good. So, we're here today to evaluate the business, dissect the books and see if we can find the leaks before it's too late, and I'm bringing you behind the scenes with me!"

Very different from a linear delivery style, but much more interesting and engaging, while still leveraging the 4-Step Video Intro system shared in Chapter 15.

Let's recap the 4 stages to creating intros that keep your viewers watching to create higher audience retention on YouTube:

➢ **Stage 1** | Open with a Known Tension

➢ **Stage 2** | Seed for a Future Resolution

➢ **Stage 3** | Showcase "The How"

➢ **Stage 4** | State the Next Logical Question(s), unanswered

If we break down the intro we crafted, leveraging creative editing techniques, we can see that all the elements are present.

➢ **Stage 1** | Open with a Known Tension

"If we keep operating at this rate, I'll be shutting down my shop by the end of the year."

➢ **Stage 2** | Seed for a Future Resolution

"... If I can't figure this out fast, this business is closing."

➢ **Stage 3** | Showcase "The How"

"I'm taking a full day to assess one of my clients who is concerned they're losing money at a rapid rate and have to find the gaps or their shop might be closing for good. So, we're here today to evaluate the business, dissect the books and see if we can find the leaks before it's too late, and I'm bringing you behind the scenes with me!"

➢ **Stage 4** | State the Next Logical Question(s), unanswered

"... and see if we can find the leaks before it's too late..."

We've now introduced creative storytelling elements by repackaging the same tips we could share in our office, but by changing the environment, introducing a character to the story, and showing Sara as the guide who gives her a plan, that leads to success to avoid failure.

You may be thinking, "That sounds awesome, Diana, but my clients aren't in my local area or my clients don't want to be seen on camera. What can I do instead?" Great question!

While there will always be clients that prefer discretion, there will always be clients willing to share their story if it will help someone else.

Because you now have a growing community online, present an offer to help a client, maybe even for free or at a discounted rate, to be featured on a future episode on the channel. There *will* be interest because, remember, you're Yoda. People value and love Yoda.

You can even do this digitally, like my friend Dale Roberts of the YouTube Channel Dale L. Roberts (formerly Self-Publishing with Dale) did in his series called Book Rescue. This series features struggling new authors desperately needing help to revamp, revive, and fix their books filled with awesome stories but often terrible book covers and poor branding that don't sell the greatness the author infused into their book.

Instead of a linear content delivery style, reviewing the book assets, and giving the same advice he would in a talking-head video, it's designed with creative storytelling elements to better capture and keep the viewers interested, while still giving his amazing advice.

And guess what? It's all done remotely, leveraging recordings of online conference calls, behind-the-scenes footage and even getting brand sponsorships from companies like Fiverr to leverage their platform to help bring this series to life.

For some, talking about "how to self-publish a book" may seem boring, but to the interested and right target audience, it's never boring because it's something they deeply desire and want to know how to do. Dale does an excellent job in his series, using creative storytelling throughout this entire series to make the character the hero, and not himself.

Throughout all the wins and sometimes less than desired results, in some instances, he remains the trusted guide so that the person he's helping comes out as the hero, as well as the viewer watching receiving value from his solutions.

This is why we love shows on networks like HGTV, The Food Network, or even some of our favorite shows on YouTube because they not only leverage creative storytelling elements that capture and keep our attention with creative storytelling but share the solutions that position the character in the show and the viewer watching, to leverage the solutions as well as the hero does.

You don't need to turn every video you create into some massive Hollywood production, but consider the video ideas you have tucked away in a journal or collecting digital dust in your favorite note editor that could be birthed to life with a twist.

When hiring a video editor, consider the primary styles of editing they will need to be skilled in and see how creative they are with their storytelling skills.

You won't be able to see how they transformed the raw content into the final video or how much of the edit is their own original idea versus their clients' input. However, you will see how they were able to bring that vision to life.

So, as you build a team, consider how they're not only able to help save you time but also to help reimagine new video ideas and become a partner in your brand versus a slave to your meticulous instructions.

Creative Freedom

Before you build a content marketing-focused dream team, you need to agree to this one thing, and that's to provide your team with creative freedom. I can't tell you the joy I've felt to see my brand elevated with the level of skill my team provides every week by getting out of their way and allowing them to have creative freedom in the projects they tackle. Our best work, to this day, has never come from my intervention, but in allowing my team to use their unique ideas to bring projects for the brand to life.

I've interviewed a lot of video editors and asked a depth of questions that allows us to really have a unique conversation that shares honest answers of their experiences with previous clients, and how many repeatedly state they wish the client would allow them to freely edit versus giving them a step-by-step must-follow instruction guide on every element in the video.

This isn't to say you can't direct your team on what you envision or set guidelines of what's on brand and what's not, but get out of the way and let them work!

Go, and mind you some business.

When you hire someone to take work off of your plate, go work on the things that only you can do.

A good video editor knows better than to make certain elementary errors in videos. When onboarding a video editor, have a brand guide of how loud your audio should be, the style of music that best represents your brand via video, and provide your video editor with the brand style guide that shares the technical elements and personality style of your brand.

After that, get out of their way and allow them creative freedom.

When you can learn to hand the reins to your video editor and trust that they know what elements are acceptable or not for the brand, you can truly begin to amplify your brand using video.

CREATOR NEXT STEPS

- [ ] How can you structure and organize your content creation folder to be more efficient?
- [ ] What is the number one creative block you should hire out in the next 30 to 60 days in your business?
- [ ] Check out the Building a Team course here: **BuildingATeam.Live**

Chapter 20

16 Months

I was so excited!

I had just moved into my new apartment after recently being promoted at my job, and I was elated.

I had bought all new furniture, kitchen gadgets, and accessories, and after setting up the new shelving systems, I went to bed that night with a pain in my side that felt awkward and sore beyond anything I had ever felt before.

I had been moving a lot of large and heavy appliances and grocery hauls to stock my cabinets, so I had been pushing myself pretty hard, but this pain was sharp and definitely grabbed my attention more than any typical sore muscle feeling. I took some medicine to hopefully relieve the pain and figured I should probably slow down and give my body a break from all this heavy lifting.

The next few mornings, it became increasingly harder to even lift my legs over the tub to get out the shower without feeling this persistently sharp pain in my side. As the weeks progressed on, the pain didn't subside but became a regular daily occurrence that became very disturbing.

Like any responsible adult adulting, I set up a doctor's appointment to see what was going on. Little did I know this would be the beginning of a revolving door in and out of hospitals and doctors' offices trying to investigate why the heck was a 20-something healthy young woman in non-stop pain for several days on end.

Days turned into weeks, and weeks turned into months. Every day at work became increasingly harder as the only solution any doctor could give me was the very strong medicine Vicodin, which made it super hard to work or do virtually anything. I started having to decide how much pain I could stand to be in if I needed to drive or when to take the medicine to function as a single woman safely.

I started having to ask to be picked up from work from my mom and dad or leave work early because I was in excruciating pain and none of the doctors, x-rays, or scans could tell me what was wrong with me or even hint at what was going on. I had long passed any timeframe of potentially pulling a muscle from moving, so I knew something was seriously wrong with me.

Sixteen months into experiencing this persistent, non-stop, and by far the most excruciating daily pain I'd ever felt before in my life, I lay in my bed one night talking to my friend at a breaking point, feeling like by the time one of these doctors identified what was wrong with me, what if it was too late?

What if it turns out to be something really serious, and without knowing it, these could be defining months in a new life journey I wasn't prepared for?

I shared with my friend, "I'm sick and tired of being poked and prodded like some animal, exposing myself at all these doctors' offices like some freak on display, which feels humiliating, to be constantly asked, 'Does it hurt here?' as they aggressively poke around. It feels like they're about to rip out my intestine.

"What if something is really wrong with me and I end up dying because they can't figure out what the heck is going on? Something is seriously wrong with me, and I hate taking all this medicine that's not solving the problem. I'm done going to doctors! If I die, then I just die. I'm sick of this!"

In a tender and calming tone, my friend replied, "Di, don't say that. You're going to be fine. What did this last doctor say when you went?"

"That he didn't know what was wrong either, but he wants to send me to another 'specialist,' that'll just probably be some other quack that says that same thing, that he doesn't know," I said with an attitude.

"Then just go and see what he says. If he doesn't know, we'll go to a doctor out of state until we can find someone that can tell you what's wrong. Somebody's got to know something! We'll figure it out!" she replied.

"Nah, I'm done going to these doctors. None of them know anything, and it just ends up being the same thing, or they think I'm drug-seeking for more medicine when I don't want to take any of this crap at all!" I replied, by now unintentionally yelling at my friend.

"Di, just go to this one last doctor, please, and see what he says, and we'll take it from there. Okay?"

I promised my friend I would make this last-ditch effort to go to yet another "specialist," but I literally had no more hope left.

About a week later, I sat staring into the doctor's eyes in disbelief that someone finally had a rational explanation of what might've caused all this grief for the last 16 months, but that was not what had me on edge. He shared with me that because of the extent of the time of non-stop pain, and visible inflammation, among other signs of concern, he told me he was issuing an emergency surgery within four days.

Four days??? I didn't know the first thing about how to prepare for surgery, what recovery would look like, or anything. I was completely out of my depth, so I did the only thing I knew to do, immediately went to talk with my mother and father and tell them what I had just learned. Despite the visible shock and concern on their faces, they came up with a game plan on how we were going to handle this, and that I'd do any recovery at their house so they can help take care of me after the surgery.

I was not even close to being prepared for what was about to happen after this surgery and was so frightened. I'd never felt fear like this before. I updated my will and told my family I loved them, afraid of what would happen. I was preparing myself in case I did not wake up from this surgery. On the outside, I kept a calm composure, but on the inside, I was a ball of nerves.

I can remember my mother and I sitting in the hospital prep room when the anesthesiologist entered the room, and he was the final step in an hours-long wait before it would be time for my surgery to begin.

I was adamant about making sure I was "aware" of when I was drifting off from the anesthesia versus just "letting them" put me under. It was the only form of resistance I could give in the battle I had already lost. When going to the various doctors, I thought there'd be a simple solution to resolve whatever was wrong with me, but surgery was not something I had even considered.

I was afraid of all of this.

What if something is seriously wrong? What if it's something they can't fix? What if I don't wake up and this is it and I can't do anything about it?

Without any notice or feeling like I was drifting off, one moment I was awake and the next moment everything was black.

I have no memory of anything, thankfully, because that's the goal with surgery, but to have a gap of time lost where there's literally just pure black, no resemblance whatsoever of being asleep, no dreams at all, just black nothingness is so bizarre.

Waking Up

I woke up in the recovery room in terrible pain and the sensation to use the restroom, but my body was literally on fire. I had never felt anything like this before in my life. This was far worse than it was before, and it was literally everywhere. I couldn't think, and even though the word "help" ran across my mind, my mouth wouldn't move.

I saw a nurse in the far-off distance across the room, but I couldn't get my words and voice to work. Somehow, after many attempts, I finally started getting a whisper of "help" to fall from my lips, and eventually, a nurse appeared by my bed, finally, to help me use the restroom.

The only problem was, this was one of those silver Lt. Dan silver bed pans from *Forrest Gump*. I looked at her like she was crazy. She made me raise up to use a bedpan, despite crying out in pain. The pain shooting through my entire body was indescribable. I could hardly get my bladder to function properly to use this thing.

Another moment of humiliation was because this nurse had a terrible attitude, and I had no energy to fight with her because some genius removed my catheter too soon.

I don't know how much time passed because I sat there in so much pain, I felt like I was going crazy. Was this normal? Are you supposed to feel this much pain after surgery??

I could hardly think straight until I finally took my focus from the square beige tiles in the ceiling down toward my feet and I saw my mother making a beeline directly toward me.

Instantly, I started weeping.

All she could do was embrace my head to console me and gently whisper in my ear, "Ann, it will be alright." Again, I don't know how much time passed because I just lost it. I didn't know how to feel other than broken.

Completely and utterly broken.

When my mother came back there, she instantly advocated for me and how much pain I was in. Another genius had messed up and didn't give me any pain medicine after the surgery, which explained why I was in excruciating pain when I woke up.

While in this recovery room, my mother produced a series of printed colored images of just what exactly was going on inside my body and why I had been in so much pain for 16 months non-stop.

Stage 4 Endometriosis with several fibroids surrounding my uterus, one embedded that couldn't be removed, and cysts growing like they owned the place. So many adhesions creating a network of webbing that flipped my appendix upside down, rotting the flesh that somehow also attached itself to my intestinal wall, pulling my intestines from their cavity.

My doctor had to pause my surgery to interrupt another doctor in the middle of surgery to quickly come to assist him with removing my appendix and reposition my intestines during my surgery. My appendix had rotted and was ready to pop my intestines, which if either the appendix or intestines had popped, both were equally fatal.

This was the news I woke up to after surgery. My fears of being at death's door were real, but I wasn't aware of just how real they were until this moment. He said a simple motion like moving my foot from the gas pedal to the brake pedal, simply driving a car, would be just enough pressure to cause either my intestines or my appendix to pop.

Hearing this after driving myself for months on end, and even driving myself to the hospital that day, I hadn't quite processed what they were saying. I couldn't say the words, though.

Finally, with a bit of sanity returning to me after getting some of the pain to subside, I was eventually moved to a private room.

I was numb.

I sat there for hours, just unsure of what to think or how to feel. I was lost. My mother and father sat with me every day during recovery and made sure I was taken care of. And I'll forever be grateful for their care during this whole process.

It wasn't until my dad handed me the phone with my oldest sister wanting to talk to me that I finally came to grips with what I was told in the recovery room a few days prior.

My sister and I talked for a short time and it was mostly just an apology because she didn't realize how serious of an issue it really was from previous conversations we'd had. She eventually asked what all exactly had happened and then the words were finally forced from my mouth. I finally said it.

"Deana, I almost died," I barely uttered out through a cracked and breaking voice.

I had finally said it. I had literally almost died, and it was in saying it aloud that made this entire experience a reality for me.

The next several weeks of recovery at my parents' house were filled with all new levels of terror from recurring fevers, unexplainable seizures, and undue stress on my poor parents, who took care of me every single day.

Living on Purpose

Despite still battling what doctors have diagnosed as an incurable disease, endometriosis has become my daily nemesis in the process to become who I was created to be.

However, I share this experience with you because just the decision alone to transition from being an entrepreneur to a content-creating entrepreneur doesn't mean life will stop throwing curveballs at us.

Being diagnosed with Stage 4 Endometriosis forever changed my life. It didn't matter that I was young and healthy. It didn't matter that I hadn't yet identified what I wanted to do with my life. It didn't matter that I hadn't achieved any of the goals I'd wanted to in life yet. My life was still almost taken from me and I had nothing to show for my 27 years of living.

What could be said of my life? I made great peach cobblers? Played with nieces and nephews? Cracked funny jokes all the time? I had done nothing with my life.

This was where my journey began with video because I was determined to make my life mean something with this second opportunity at living. It was at this moment I prayed and asked God to help reveal to me my purpose in life, and within a few weeks after returning to work, I found myself listening to podcasts and watching YouTube videos about creating online content for your business. This would eventually uncover my passion for simplifying video content creation and helping other entrepreneurs share their vision using video.

You never know where your viewers are coming from in their lives when they land on your videos and how it can help literally transform and help change their lives.

Never discredit the value your content can bring to someone's life because they could be someone like I was back in 2015 getting a second opportunity to live and looking for answers.

Value the solutions you provide.

They matter.

CREATOR NEXT STEPS

- [ ] Identify the real reason why you're building your brand, and why video is a must-have in your business.
- [ ] **What legacy do you want to create with life?** Really take some time and ask what you want from life, and how video will help your achieve it.

Chapter 21

The Next Logical Step

As you're well on your way to becoming a content creation master as you finish this book, there's one final strategy I want to teach you that's been seeded throughout this entire book: Learn & Do.

This is the best way to avoid creative constipation that sends you into an analysis paralysis loop of wishing to create a video but never actually creating a video because you feel like you need to learn one more thing, buy one more piece of gear or watch one more tutorial.

As the Queen of Video Simplified, allow me to release you from this infinite loop of excuses to enter the prosperous land of **Learn & Do**.

When you learn something new, go and execute it.

When you're finished watching a tutorial on how to do something, go test it out or follow along in real-time with the video to put what you're learning to work.

The greatest gift I can receive as an educator is seeing my students execute things they've learned from my content and trainings, and now, this book.

Now that you've learned how to transform the ideas in your mind into our content from boring and bland videos viewers would skip, to videos they're engaged in and excited to binge-watch, my hope for you is that you'll continue to create content that educates, inspires, and changes people's lives to share your vision with the world.

The One Right Video can transform your life and the lives of the people you touch.

Go, and create for the people that need you.

Learn & Do.

CREATOR NEXT STEPS

- [ ] Book a call and get a jump-start on your video content creation here: OneRightVideo.com/NextSteps

Thank You For Reading My Book!

I really appreciate all of your feedback and I love hearing what you have to say.

I need your input to make the next version of this book and my future books better.

Please take 2 minutes now and leave a review on Amazon to help fellow entrepreneurs find this book: OneRightVideo.com/Review

Thank you so much!

~ **DIANA GLADNEY**

VIDEO SIMPLIFIED PODCAST
w/ Diana Gladney
READY FOR MORE SIMPLIFIED STRATEGIES TO AMPLIFY YOUR BRAND?
Subscribe to the Video Simplified Podcast
Listen on Apple Podcasts
Listen on Google Podcasts
Listen on amazon music
LISTEN ON Spotify
NEW EPISODES EVERY WEEK!
VideoSimplifiedPodcast.com

1. Ceci, L. "Hours of Video Uploaded to YouTube Every Minute." Statista, 9 Jan. 2023, www.statista.com/statistics/259477/hours-of-video-uploaded-to-youtube-every-minute.
2. "CDC: 1 in 4 US Adults Live with a Disability." Centers for Disease Control and Prevention, Centers for Disease Control and Prevention, 16 Aug. 2018, https://www.cdc.gov/media/releases/2018/p0816-disability.html.
3. "Understand Key Moments for Audience Retention." Google Support, Support.Google.com, 2023, https://support.google.com/youtube/answer/9314415?hl=en. Accessed 7 July 2022.
4. Miller, Donald. "Chapter 2/Story in a Nutshell." Building a Storybrand: Clarify Your Message so Customers Will Listen, HarperCollins Leadership, an Imprint of HarperCollins, New York, NY, 2017, pp. 20–20.

Made in United States
Cleveland, OH
04 November 2026

47642875R00126